¡Viva México!

A journey through food, fiestas and beyond

DK EYEWITNESS

¡Viva México!

A journey through food, fiestas and beyond

CONTENTS

¡BIENVENIDO a MÉXICO!

If you spent a lifetime travelling through Mexico, you'd scarcely scratch the surface. It's the largest Spanish-speaking country in the world. Its history stretches back thousands of years to the great Mesoamerican empires. It forms a physical and cultural bridge between North and Central America, with landscapes encompassing snowy peaks, golden deserts and tropical rainforests, and with each state home to an array of languages, cuisines and climates.

Yet the country's complexities have meant it's often misrepresented. Stories of conflict and corruption mean Mexico's darker side can obscure its light, while certain beloved icons of Mexico – think tacos, tequila and sombreros – have been used to commodify its rich culture. In its sheer scale and diversity, Mexico defies simple definitions.

¡Viva México! is here to celebrate the country's huge tapestry, bringing you closer to Mexico's glorious landscapes, traditional dishes and cultural touchstones. In themed chapters, you'll discover how history informs the present: from Indigenous communities celebrating their ties to the land to huge Catholic festivals in beautiful churches. You'll also learn how Day of the Dead traditions vary from region to region, how staples of Mexican food have changed as they've travelled the globe and how pioneering film-makers continue to influence global cinema.

By the end you'll have fallen in love with this wonderful country as much as we have. As proud Mexicans cry aloud during the country's annual Independence Day festivities: *"¡Viva México!"* Long live Mexico!

Above A farmer riding through fields of agave in Jalisco

Right Busy streets during Independence Day celebrations in the city of Guanajuato

INtRoDUCiNG MeXiCo

To get to know Mexico, you first need to understand its sheer size and diversity. This vast country is one of the largest in the Americas, with a varied geography that stretches from white-sand beaches on the coast to smoking volcanoes in the interior. These landscapes have witnessed the rise and fall of Mesoamerican empires, the arrival of the Spanish and the advent of the modern-day nation, forged from rebellion and revolution. Great swathes of the country remain agricultural, and are home to rural communities that sustain themselves on the bounty of the land. But Mexico has also become increasingly urbanized, with dynamic cities spreading across the country. It's this glorious diversity that's helped to build the nation and make Mexico what it is today.

ON THE MAP

STATES OF MEXICO

Mexico, known officially as the United Mexican States, sits in southern North America and has a population of almost 130 million. More than half the population live close to the capital, Mexico City, with the north and south sparsely settled. Sprawling over more than 760,000 sq miles (1,900,000 sq km), it's the fifth-largest country in the Americas and the fourteenth-largest in the world by landmass. Mexico comprises 32 states spanning four time zones; here are the highlights.

Chihuahua, in northern Mexico, is the country's largest state, with a population of almost 3.8 million. It sits on a plain that dips to meet the Rio Grande. The state is known for its cattle ranching industry and the heritage of the Rarámuri people.

Jalisco, located in western Mexico, is home to almost 9 million people. The state stands out as the birthplace of mariachi *(p125)* and tequila *(p108)*, though its rich cultural heritage includes other quintessentially Mexican traditions like the *El son de la negra* and *El jarabe tapatío* dances.

Baja California in northern Mexico sits at the top of a long, narrow peninsula on the edge of the Sonoran Desert. Its capital city, Mexicali, lies on the border with the US, opposite Calexico, California. The region has a thriving agriculture and fishing industry, and a population of around 3.8 million.

Nuevo León is one of Mexico's most affluent states, due to its industrial prowess, with Monterrey, the state's largest city, home to ironworks and a vast textile industry. The arid climate and desert landscapes in the north of the state contrast starkly with the mountain slopes and subtropical valleys of the south.

The state of **Campeche** in the Yucatán Peninsula sits on the edge of the Gulf of Mexico. The state, along with the other states in the Yucatán Peninsula – Yucatán and Quintana Roo – possesses rich Mayan heritage, with Campeche home to archaeological sites like Calakmul within the Calakmul Biosphere Reserve.

The **State of Mexico** (sometimes referred to as Edomex to distinguish it from the name of the country as a whole) is the country's most densely populated state. The territory was historically the heartland of the sprawling Aztec Empire, and today it surrounds the capital, Mexico City.

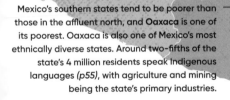

Mexico's southern states tend to be poorer than those in the affluent north, and **Oaxaca** is one of its poorest. Oaxaca is also one of Mexico's most ethnically diverse states. Around two-fifths of the state's 4 million residents speak Indigenous languages (*p55*), with agriculture and mining being the state's primary industries.

LANDSCAPES

Mexico is more like a small continent than a single country, with magnificent terrain encompassing rainforests, mangrove lagoons, deserts, coastal reefs and snowy peaks.

Across its vast and dramatic landmass, Mexico is home to a spectacular array of landscapes and climates. Situated between the US and Central America, with the Tropic of Cancer cutting through the state of Baja California, Mexico generally has a dry and arid desert climate in the north while the south is considered tropical.

DESERT AND SCRUBLAND
Over half of Mexico's land is arid, with vast scrubland taking up swathes of the country, particularly in the north. The

Sonoran Desert, which is the hottest in Mexico, drags its dusty tongue over most of the Baja California peninsula and the state of Sonora, east of the Gulf of California. Its cousin, the Chihuahuan Desert, is found a little further to the east, with heavier rains nurturing rippling grasslands and colourful endemic cacti, creating a postcard vision of the Mexican desert, with vast mountains rising in the distance.

MOUNTAINS AND HIGHLANDS
A series of jagged mountain ranges run the length of Mexico, and around half the country is at least 1,000 m (3,200 ft) above sea level. In the centre, the Central Mexican Plateau is sandwiched between two mountain ranges: the Sierra Madre Occidental to the west and the Sierra Madre Oriental in the east. Within the Sierra Madre Occidental, the Sierra del Tigre range is famous for its unique "sky islands": mountains with drastically

Left The Chihuahuan Desert in northern Mexico, home to 2,000 species of plant

Right Copper Canyon in the Sierra Madre Occidental mountain range

different habitats in their upper reaches compared to their lowlands. Rich alluvial and volcanic soils with regular rainfall means the plateau between these ranges acts as the country's *tortilleria* – it produces 60 per cent of Mexico's maize and a large proportion of its avocados.

The highlands and gorges of the Filo Mayor mountains in the southern state of Guerrero are dotted with red and purple opium poppies. The country's wildly profitable heroin trade starts here, with impoverished farmers supplying opium paste to the cartels.

In the northeast, the Sierra Madre Oriental mountains contain the country's tallest peak and the third tallest in North America, the dormant volcano Pico de Orizaba. The range plunges into the azure waters of the Mexican Riviera.

COASTLINE AND WETLANDS

Mexico's coastline totals over 10,000 km (6,250 miles). On the Pacific side to the west and south, the coast is defined by islets and rocky promontories like those on the Sea of Cortés. This vast stretch of turquoise water is fondly known as "the world's aquarium" and is beloved by whale sharks looking for a sheltered spot to birth their young. The coastline of the Baja California peninsula in the northwest is one of the country's most biodiverse, while the coastal Yucatán Peninsula in the southeast separates the shimmering, emerald waters and golden beaches of the Caribbean Sea from the vast Gulf of Mexico.

Further inland, Mexico's delicate wetland habitats range from mangrove swamps to saline lagoons. Mexico's mangrove forests, like those at the Chacahua lagoon in the south, are among the world's most productive ecosystems. The roots of the mangroves, submerged

in brackish coastal water, act as nesting sites for young fish and crustaceans, while their branches are home to birds and monkeys. These forests are under stark threat, however, due largely to warming seas and coastal development. Coastal populations like those in the Yucatán Peninsula are working tirelessly to restore these landscapes by planting and nurturing mangroves.

RAINFORESTS AND JUNGLES

Mexico's tropical rainforests have faced similar challenges, with less than 10 per cent of original rainforest still standing. The largest remaining rainforest in North America is the mighty Lacandón, which stretches from Chiapas into Guatamala. The Lacandón contains over 30 per cent of all Mexican bird species and 25 per cent of its

mammal species. The huge Usumacinta River snakes past the southern edge of the Lacandón, flanked by ancient Mayan ruins like the city of Yaxchilán.

Vast forests are also found across the Yucatán Peninsula. Exploring the Peninsula's interior is like being immersed in a Mayan creation myth and, indeed, this region was the heartland of this ancient civilization. Every so often, ruins such as the pyramids of Chichén Itzá (p37)and Calakmul emerge from the tropical jungle. More than 6,000 cenotes – unique sinkholes that plunge deep into the region's limestone crust, leading to a network of underground rivers – were believed to be the entrance to the underworld by the country's Indigenous peoples.

Mexico's Warming Seas

A warming climate could have devastating effects on Mexico's coastal settlements and ecosystems. The Gulf of Mexico has seen water temperatures rise far faster than the global average, threatening the precarious livelihoods of communities along the coast. Flooding, for example, has doubled in frequency over the last ten years. Climate scientists are looking to the Gulf to better understand the effects of warming seas, while local activists are pushing for increased investment in climate-resilient coastal infrastructure.

FLORA AND FAUNA

With such abundant landscapes, it's little wonder that Mexico lays claim to over 10 per cent of the world's known species and almost every type of natural habitat. Here are some of the country's rarest and most magnificent inhabitants.

AXOLOTL

Incredibly cute but desperately endangered, the axolotl is so beloved in Mexico that when it was launched as the "face" of the 50 peso note, people refused to spend them. Endemic only to the canals of Xochimilco in Mexico City and once part of the Aztec diet, there are few left in the wild; however, numerous conservation efforts are underway to preserve this species of salamander.

CACTUS

Cacti in Mexico come in all shapes and sizes; in fact, close to half of the world's cacti can be found in Mexico – and the majority of those are endemic to the country. From the towering *saguaros* of the Sonoran Desert in the north, to the prickly pear producing *nopales* – the paddles of which are also consumed – to the diminutive potted varietals thriving on sunny windowsills across the country, these spiky plants are rooted (literally) in both the country and culture.

XOLOITZCUINTLE

Often referred to as "hairless Mexican dogs", *xolos* – as they're known colloquially – are associated with the Chichimeca god of death, Xólotl, and have been revered since Mesoamerican times, when they were believed to guide souls through Mictlán, the City of Death. In Mexico, they're sometimes seen as pets, dressed in cosy sweaters or embroidered *blusas* to keep them warm.

JACARANDAS

Though not endemic to Mexico, the blossoming branches of the iconic lilac jacaranda trees are a sight to behold each spring in Mexico City. Introduced to Mexico during Porfirio Díaz's presidency in the 20th century by a Japanese gardener who fell into favour with the president, jacarandas are now symbolic of the capital and can be found flourishing on main streets across the city.

GOLDEN EAGLE

Eagle iconography dates back to the Aztec Empire, and the golden eagle – or, simply, "Mexican eagle" – continues to sit at the heart of Mexican identity (and the country's flag), a symbol of strength and courage. Mexico City football team Club América even has an eagle mascot called Celeste who appears before every game. In the wild, you're more likely to spot golden eagles in the dry, arid reaches of the northern and central states.

1 The axolotl, with feathery gills and webbed feet

2 A *nopal* cactus, commonly used in Mexican cuisine

3 The unique and furless xoloitzcuintle

4 Purple blossom of the jacaranda tree

5 A golden eagle, a symbol of Mexican identity

MONARCH BUTTERFLY

Every winter, monarch butterflies make their annual migration from the upper reaches of North America back to the embrace of Central Mexico's humid forests. Considered by some Indigenous communities to be the souls of the dead returning, the butterflies make for an impressive spectacle, colouring the skies and trees orange, branches bending beneath their collective weight. And although threatened by logging, even in the protected reaches of Mexico's Monarch Butterfly Biosphere Reserve, the butterflies endure.

CEMPASÚCHIL

Known in English as Mexican marigolds, *cempasúchiles* (taken from the Nahuatl *cempōhualxōchitl*) are most strongly associated with the Day of the Dead and cultivated primarily in Central Mexico. Their strong scent and soft petals – most commonly deep orange in colour – serve to help guide the dead back to the land of the living. Beyond Día de los Muertos altars, endemic-to-Mexico *cempasúchiles* are used to colour textiles, relieve indigestion and flavour ice cream.

AGAVE AZUL

Closely related to the thorny mezcal-making maguey – all agaves are actually types of maguey – the blue agave is the plant to thank for top-shelf tequila *(p108)*. Native to and cultivated principally in the state of Jalisco, as well as Colima, Nayarit and Aguascalientes, this enormous plant comprises fleshy but sharp-edged *pencas* (leaves) and a *piña* (heart), the distilled juices of which are used to create tequila. You can also create a range of textiles (including vegan leathers) and syrups with the *pencas* and core, respectively.

JAGUAR

The bewhiskered, snarling face of the jaguar is replicated in masks and mythology across Mexico, depicted in the *danza de los tecuanes* (Dance of the Jaguars), and present in Zapotec, Mayan and Aztec cultures. Considered spirit guides to some and sacred gods to others, the jaguar – the Americas' largest feline – is most commonly found prowling the vast plains and shaded jungles of the Yucatán Peninsula.

AHUEHUETE

While the country's most iconic example of an *ahuehuete*, or Cypress tree, can be found in the tiny Oaxacan village of Santa María del Tule – the *árbol del Tule* has a near 45-m (150-ft) circumference and is thought to be more than 2,000 years old – you'll find these mammoths anywhere there's enough water to sustain them. As one popular legend goes, it was beneath an *ahuehuete* – the national tree of Mexico – where colonizer Hernán Cortés wept after losing a decisive battle against the Mexicas in the Valley of Mexico.

6 Monarch butterflies fluttering between branches

7 Mexican marigolds, the iconic flower of the Day of the Dead

8 Giant blue agave plants growing in the desert of Guadalajara

9 A jaguar stalking in the undergrowth

10 Mexico's national tree, the *ahuehuete*, or Montezuma bald cypress

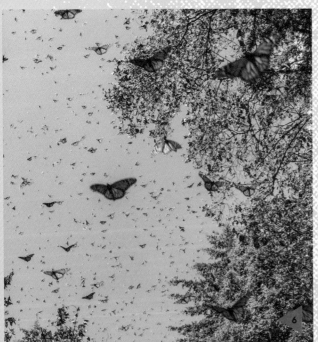

6

7

8

9

10

COAT *of* ARMS

In Mexico, flora and fauna hold great cultural significance, both as symbols of national identity and in Indigenous lore. The Mexican coat of arms, which appears prominently on Mexico's flag, reflects this significance. Portraying an eagle sitting atop a prickly pear cactus holding a snake in its beak, the national emblem harks back to the foundation myth of Tenochtitlán, the Aztec capital before the arrival of the Spanish.

Legend has it that the Aztecs left Aztlán, a town believed to have been in northwestern Mexico, in search of a place to start a new life. Huitzilopochtli, the Aztec god of the sun and war, instructed the Aztec peoples to settle wherever they saw an eagle sitting on a cactus devouring a snake. After wandering through inhospitable lands, they arrived at the Valley of Mexico in around 1325 and spotted the sign they were seeking. The eagle sat on a small island in the middle of Lake Texcoco and it was here that the city of Tenochtitlán was founded. The vast city was conquered by Spanish conquistadors a couple of centuries later and eventually became Mexico City.

The national emblem has adorned Mexico's flag since 1968. The flag's colours (green, white and red) haven't changed since 1821 but their meaning has evolved over time. Originally, green represented independence, white stood for religion and red for union. The Mexican state has been secular since the mid-19th century, and the colours now stand for hope, unity and the blood of heroes who fought for independence.

RURal LIVING

For thousands of years, Mexicans have had a deep relationship to the land – a tie that continues to this day. Away from the cities, rural communities have formed strong bonds to weather the challenges of country life.

Since the days of the Aztec Empire, when ancient inhabitants developed rich farming practices, agriculture – and therefore rural living – has been central to Mexico's culture and economy.

EARLY COMMUNITIES
Rural life for the Aztecs was defined by ingenuity and adaptation. A host of innovative agricultural practices were

developed, including the use of floating farms which allowed vegetables to be grown on marshy land in the Valley of Mexico. Though the Aztec Empire was formed of three city-states with a large urban population (the capital, Tenochtitlán, had 200,000 inhabitants), the Aztec countryside was itself highly complex. A patchwork of small, rural communities dotted the landscape,

Above Stacked crops atop a ploughed field in central Mexico

Above left Aztec floating farms depicted in an illustration (c 1900)

managed by a rural class known as the *mācēhualtin*. These communities weren't entirely isolated from the cities: they engaged in long-distance trade with the urban centres, and their agricultural output was necessary to provide for the urban population.

The country's agricultural communities have continued to play a key social role in Mexico over the centuries. This was highlighted after Mexico gained independence from Spain in 1821, when 50 per cent of the labour force worked in the agricultural sector, and farming became a key economic driver for the modern nation.

LIVING ON THE LAND

Increasing urbanization and the lure of the country's cities (and the education and employment opportunities that come with them) have led to a dwindling rural population. This began following the Mexican Revolution (*p40*): agrarian reforms promoted after the conflict saw many farmers freed from semi-feudal systems which had kept them bound to the land. Landowners, who suddenly lacked cheap labour, began moving their investments from the countryside towards flourishing cities. As a result, the country's urban population increased, to the cost of rural communities.

In 1950, more than half of Mexicans lived in rural areas; by 2020, just 21 per cent did. According to the Mexican government, nearly four out of 10 Mexican rural workers today are over 60 years old.

For those who remain in Mexico's vast rural landscapes, agriculture is still the main source of employment. The nature of rural life depends on the region, with Mexico's more sparsely populated north home to larger, industrial farms, and the south to smaller, family-owned farms. Many continue to use techniques passed down through generations, including ploughing the earth using oxen and using the milpa crop system *(p81)*.

RURAL CHALLENGES

A shrinking rural population isn't the only challenge in the countryside. Rural communities face a lack of access to healthcare, education and other

services, as well as basic infrastructure like roads and electricity. These issues exacerbate rural poverty: according to the Mexican government, as of 2018, more than half of Mexicans living in rural areas were considered poor, compared to about 38 per cent of those living in cities. The Mexican government has made some efforts to address this inequality, including increasing subsidies for farmers and instituting programmes such as *"Sembrando Vida"* ("Sowing Life"), which pays farmers to plant trees in small plots of land.

Many of these issues disproportionately affect Indigenous communities, over half of whom live in rural areas, due in part to their ancestral ties to the land and a greater emphasis on traditional livelihoods like farming. As of 2018, nearly 70 per cent of rural Indigenous people lived in poverty, with almost 30 per cent living in extreme poverty. Despite some government efforts, unemployment in these communities remains widespread, leading many Indigenous Mexicans – especially men – to migrate in search of work to other states, larger cities or even to the US.

Rural Mexico also tends to be more socially conservative than its urban centres, including when it comes to machismo attitudes *(p58)*. This is particularly true in relation to gender roles: men in rural Mexico are much more likely to be the breadwinners working out in the field, while women largely perform domestic tasks like cooking, cleaning and child-rearing.

COMMUNITY CULTURE

Despite their many challenges, rural communities in Mexico enjoy a dynamic cultural life. Throughout the year, a host of seasonal festivals and celebrations are

Above A parade of charros (cowboys), part of the *charrería*

Left Harvesting beans in rural Oaxaca

are focal points for the entire community, while traditional sports like the *charrería (p144)* continue to draw large crowds. Gatherings are largely dictated by the agricultural calendar, reflecting a close connection to the rhythms of the land. Among these is the Santa Cruz festival in early May, when many Indigenous communities celebrate the start of the rainy season. But Indigenous festivities in Mexico extend far beyond venerating the land: from exuberant Day of the Dead celebrations in Janitzio, in the state of Michoacán, to the soaring *voladores de Papantla* (fliers of Papantla) in Veracruz *(p72)*, it's in Mexico's rural towns and villages where the country's vibrant cultural traditions feel most alive.

Muxes

While Mexico's larger cities tend to be more progressive, and therefore more accepting of the country's LGBTQ+ community, rural areas also have a part to play. In rural Oaxaca state, the Indigenous Zapotec community is known for its *muxes*, people who are assigned male at birth but who take on female gender roles as they grow older. Embodying a third gender that is neither strictly male nor female, *muxes* are widely accepted by Zapotec communities.

URBaN Lifestyles

Despite a deeply rooted rural culture, some eight out of 10 Mexicans now live in cities, and the country's dynamic urban centres are hotbeds of culture and industry.

While traditional conceptions of Mexico might paint the country as largely rural, it's now highly urbanized, with a quarter of the population living in just three areas: Mexico City, Guadalajara and Monterrey. This process has taken place over many decades as people from all over Mexico have migrated from rural areas to bigger cities in search of economic opportunity.

EXPANDING CITIES

Like in many other countries around the world, urbanization has changed the nature of society in Mexico. This change gathered pace during the second half of the 20th century, with industrialization providing greater economic opportunities in cities, as well as the growth of schools and universities in urban areas. This led to the country's cities expanding at a rapid rate.

By far the biggest population boom took place in Mexico City, which became not just the nation's political capital, but also its economic heart, home to vast industries such as textiles manufacturing, retail and banking, which took root across the wider metropolitan area. In 1930, Mexico City had a population of just over 1 million people, which tripled by 1950 and ballooned to more than 9 million by 1970. Today, the Mexico City metropolitan area is home to more than 20 million people, making it one of

Left Crowds of people on Avenida Francisco I Madero in Mexico City

Right The city of Guanajuato in central Mexico

the largest cities in the world. Beyond this metropolis, Mexico has 16 cities that are home to over 1 million people each, including Guadalajara in the west and Monterrey in the north, each with more than 5 million inhabitants.

Cities close to the border experienced a particular boom after the signing of the North American Free Trade Agreement (NAFTA) in 1994, which rapidly expanded trade between the US and Mexico. Factories producing everything from electronics to jeans suddenly sprang up all along the border, attracting new residents in search of higher-paying, steadier jobs. The population of cities like Tijuana, Ciudad Juárcz and Reynosa grew by 50 per cent in the years after the trade agreement was signed.

CITY STRUGGLES

As these cities grew, the divide between rich and poor grew with it. Many of the rural poor who moved to the city set up informal settlements on the peripheries of large metropolises. Despite the greater job opportunities offered in urban centres, wages in Mexico have been historically low, particularly in the informal sector (including family-owned restaurants and street vendors), and poverty in cities is widespread. Many settlements on the outskirts of cities are lacking in basic services like running water, and also have high rates of violent crime and corruption.

Large cities, such as the capital, also highlight Mexico's sharp class divisions, with wealthy enclaves and elite gated communities just a stone's throw away from impoverished neighbourhoods. One such example is the business district of Santa Fe in Mexico City, which sits next to a deprived area. The Mexican writer Carlos Fuentes famously called Mexico City the "capital of under-development" in the 1980s, highlighting the city's notorious poverty and lack of social investment. Class divisions across urban centres are still steep: in Mexico

STORIES FROM MEXICO

My name is Ramiro Maravilla. I was born in Mexico City, but I lived part of my childhood in a town called Ario de Rayón in Michoacán state. Something I remember about Ario de Rayón is always being woken up by animal noises: there were roosters, sheep, a lot of dogs barking. I also remember that you could see the stars. In Mexico City when you looked up you couldn't see the stars, but in Michoacán you could look up at the sky and see so many stars.

I moved back to Mexico City when I was seven and I'm really used to it because I was born here. I'm especially accustomed to having access to almost everything. In Mexico City you have all the government institutions, all the universities. Also, in Michoacán there really isn't an LGBTQ+ life, so it would have been really hard to come out as gay. Mexico City is like a paradise: we started LGBTQ+ legislation, gay marriage, adoption, we have Mexico City Pride. This is where the movement began.

Ramiro Maravilla, Mexico City

City's outer borough of Milpa Alta, more than 50 per cent of people are considered poor, according to government figures, compared to less than 8 per cent in the wealthy inner borough of Miguel Hidalgo, home to the affluent Polanco neighbourhood.

EFFORTS TO MODERNIZE

Despite their problems, Mexico's cities remain dynamic places, which are improving thanks to increased government investment. An expanding middle class is reaping the benefits of substantial incomes, better education and higher-quality homes. Though many communities still lag behind, efforts are underway to improve living conditions in working-class boroughs, too. In the working-class Iztapalapa borough of Mexico City, the mayor has installed bright streetlights to improve security and built giant parks with public swimming pools, sports fields, theatres and other facilities to improve access to recreation, art and other activities.

Mexico City has also transformed its public transit infrastructure, as a way to tackle vehicle congestion and air pollution. Successive city governments have expanded the capital's sprawling underground subway system and added new modes of transport, including the successful urban bus line known as the "metrobus"; cable cars that have greatly reduced commuter times; and an ever-expanding bike sharing programme. Government policies, including stricter

vehicle emissions standards, have greatly reduced pollution; from being named the world's most polluted city by the UN in 1992, Mexico City now ranks as 917th.

FORWARD-THINKING CITIES

Many of the rural migrants who arrived in cities at the start of the 20th century were steeped in the egalitarian ideologies of the Mexican Revolution (*p40*), which laid the foundation for cities as progressive urban centres. The capital was one of the first major cities in the Americas to legalize same-sex marriage in 2010, while also allowing abortion years before other Mexican states followed suit.

The city remains the epicentre of important protest movements, particularly Mexico's resurgent feminist movement, which has reignited in response to surging levels of violence against women. During mass protests in

Above International Women's Day march in Mexico City

Right A café in central Mexico City, popular with students

2021, feminist activists climbed a plinth in Mexico City's Paseo de la Reforma and installed a statue of a woman holding her fist to the sky as a symbol of feminist solidarity. In 2023, the council formally voted to make the statue permanent.

Mexican cities have also become centres of innovation, thanks to growing financial and business sectors, and to an influx of young people attending the country's colleges and universities. Mexico City's Universidad Nacional Autónoma de México (UNAM) is one of Latin America's most esteemed universities, and the capital has also become one of the leading technological centres in Latin America. The city of Monterrey, meanwhile, is known as an industrial hub.

BASTIONS OF CULTURE

The country's cities are more than centres of industry: they are also hubs of leisure and culture. The capital is home to more than 140 museums and dozens of galleries – including the monumental Museo de Antropología e Historia – as well as concert halls, cinemas and some of the world's best restaurants. But other cities don't skimp on cultural offerings either: Guadalajara, for instance, is famed for its mariachi music and gastronomy and also hosts the Guadalajara International Book Fair – the most important in the Spanish-speaking world. Even smaller cities are known for their cultural flair, with Morelia in western Mexico hosting one of the country's most important film festivals, and Guanajuato hosting the International Cervantino Festival every year, showcasing literature, dance, music and other art forms.

Digital Nomads

Mexico's cities have become increasingly attractive places to live, not just for Mexicans but for people around the world. The rise of working from home, particularly during the COVID-19 pandemic, led to a surge in so-called digital nomads moving to Mexico City's desirable central neighbourhoods. Although this has boosted local economies, it has also caused a backlash from longtime residents. The city government has made some efforts to mitigate this, such as constructing housing for local residents, and has plans to limit private real estate developments.

Mexico's largest border city, **Tijuana** is home to the world's busiest land border crossing, leading to San Diego in the US. Historically one of the world's most dangerous cities, with cartels vying for control of the drug trade, it's now home to a vibrant urban art scene.

ON THE MAP

MAIN CITIES

Mexico's thriving cities continue to draw new arrivals from all over the world. The country's mix of climate and terrain, coupled with centuries of global immigration, have created urban centres of great cultural and architectural variety. South of the capital, cities like Puebla are defined by a heady mix of European and Indigenous influences, while in the north wealthy centres like Guadalajara are bastions of industry and manufacturing. Here are a few of the country's great cities.

Guadalajara is the capital of Jalisco in the west of central Mexico, and is Mexico's second-largest city by population. It's known for tequila, mariachi music and *tortas ahogadas,* bread filled with pork, all of which are proudly celebrated in the state of Jalisco.

One of the oldest continuously inhabited cities in the world, **Mexico City**, the nation's capital, sits in the Valley of Mexico. The huge metropolitan population (over 20 million) constitutes almost one-sixth of Mexico's total. The city encompasses central districts like Miguel Hidalgo and working-class districts like Iztapalapa in the east.

The capital of the state of Nuevo León in northeastern Mexico, **Monterrey** is known as an economic powerhouse, due in part to its proximity to the US border. The city is home to the Monterrey Institute of Technology, which has close ties to the country's business elite.

The colonial capital of **Puebla** is spread across the foothills of the Sierra Madre, southeast of Mexico City. In the colonial era, the city was a key military stronghold, and colonial architecture is still seen in the city's centre (now designated a UNESCO World Heritage Site). The city enjoys a lively mix of Indigenous and European traditions.

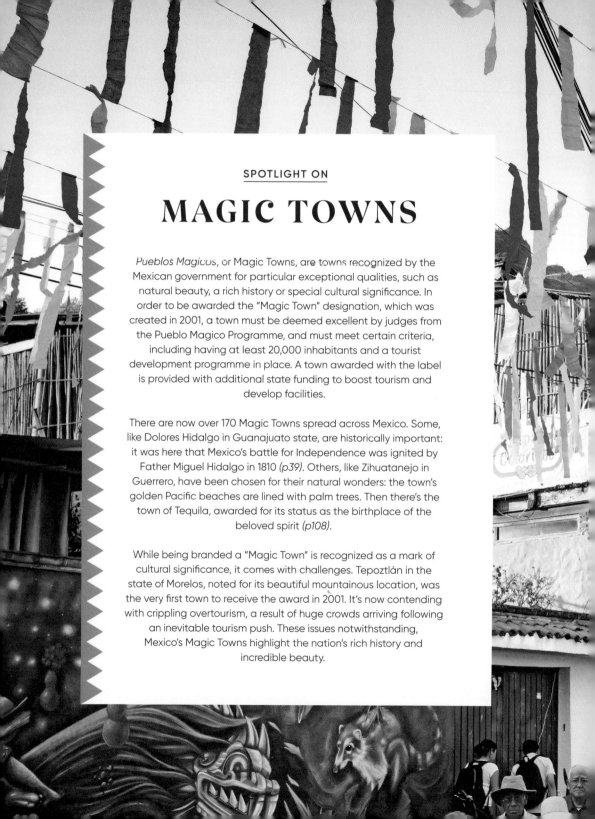

MAGIC TOWNS

Pueblos Magicos, or Magic Towns, are towns recognized by the Mexican government for particular exceptional qualities, such as natural beauty, a rich history or special cultural significance. In order to be awarded the "Magic Town" designation, which was created in 2001, a town must be deemed excellent by judges from the Pueblo Magico Programme, and must meet certain criteria, including having at least 20,000 inhabitants and a tourist development programme in place. A town awarded with the label is provided with additional state funding to boost tourism and develop facilities.

There are now over 170 Magic Towns spread across Mexico. Some, like Dolores Hidalgo in Guanajuato state, are historically important: it was here that Mexico's battle for Independence was ignited by Father Miguel Hidalgo in 1810 *(p39)*. Others, like Zihuatanejo in Guerrero, have been chosen for their natural wonders: the town's golden Pacific beaches are lined with palm trees. Then there's the town of Tequila, awarded for its status as the birthplace of the beloved spirit *(p108)*.

While being branded a "Magic Town" is recognized as a mark of cultural significance, it comes with challenges. Tepoztlán in the state of Morelos, noted for its beautiful mountainous location, was the very first town to receive the award in 2001. It's now contending with crippling overtourism, a result of huge crowds arriving following an inevitable tourism push. These issues notwithstanding, Mexico's Magic Towns highlight the nation's rich history and incredible beauty.

BRief History of Mexico

Mexico's tumultuous history spans millennia, stretching from the arrival of nomadic groups through the great Mesoamerican empires and on to the birth of a modern nation.

The long history of Mexico is a story of powerful empires, bloody invasions and seismic revolutions. Through it all, the country's diverse peoples have been innovating, carving out a remarkable nation and changing the world around them in the process.

IN THE BEGINNING

Mexico's earliest history is shrouded in mystery. It began millennia ago, after nomadic groups originating in northeast Asia crossed the Bering Strait and moved into what is now referred to as Mesoamerica. The earliest known civilization in Mexico was the Olmecs, who lived in the Gulf of Mexico from around 1500 to 400 BCE. Evidence of their proficiency in architecture can be seen in the colossal carved stone heads, thrones and stela (upright slabs) that they left behind. During the first millennium BC, however, the Olmecs declined, for reasons that are unknown.

DEVELOPING CIVILIZATIONS

It's believed the Olmecs influenced subsequent Mesoamerican civilizations that reigned in Mexico, including the Mayans, who lived in the south. The peak of the Mayan civilization came between 200 and 800 CE. The Mayans built vast pyramids and temples, and developed a written language, which included hieroglyphs. However, this civilization too declined, in around 900 CE, due to a fatal mix of civil wars, overpopulation and migration.

During the Mayan era in the Valley of Mexico, a great city-state, known as Teotihuacán, was built by unknown founders. When the city declined due to outside attacks, internal descent and poverty, a series of militarized successor states rose up to fill its place, most notably the Toltecs, who settled in the Valley of Mexico prior to the 10th century. Just like the Mayans before them, the Toltecs were eventually defeated by rival groups.

ASCENT OF THE AZTECS

The Toltecs were followed by the Aztecs, who arrived in the Valley of Mexico at the start of the 13th century. They established their capital, Tenochtitlán *(p20),*

Right The Temple of Kukulcán, built by the Mayans at Chichén Itzá

IMPORTANT
MESOAMERICAN RUINS

Monte Albán
Once the capital of the Zapotec nation, Monte Albán was built on top of a vast mountain located just outside of Oaxaca City in southern Mexico.

Teotihuacán
Meaning "the place where the gods were created", iconic Teotihuacán features two pyramids, the Temple of the Sun and the Temple of the Moon.

Chichén Itzá
The Mayan city-state of Chichén Itzá was one of the most sacred sites of the Mesoamerican era. It was designated a UNESCO World Heritage Site in 1988.

Tulum
It's no surprise the Mayans built one of their last cities in Tulum: sitting on a seaside cliff that overlooks the Mayan Riviera, the ruin's beauty is nothing short of divine.

in 1325 on several islands in the middle of Lake Texcoco, creating a vast city complete with aqueducts, canals and pyramids. Over the following centuries, the Aztecs built a strong military empire and by the 15th century many other city-states in the region were under their control. They also developed advanced religious, social, economic and educational systems, and kept time with a 364-day solar calendar.

In 1519, Spanish conquistador Hernán Cortés and his men landed in Mexico in the hope of finding gold, silver and other resources. By now, the Aztecs faced internal dissidence, overpopulation and resistance from outlying states. Joining forces with one rival state, the Spanish were able to secure control of a badly damaged Tenochtitlán in 1521, and a new city, Mexico City, was built atop the ruins.

Cortés and the Aztecs

When Cortés arrived in Mexico in 1519, he was originally met with warmth by Moctezuma, the Aztec ruler. Moctezuma's gifts of gold, however, vindicated Spanish suspicions that the area was rich in resources, and the ruler was taken prisoner. Working in alliance with some 200,000 warriors from the Tlaxcala and Cempoala city-states, the Spanish army held Tenochtitlán under siege for 93 days in 1521. Within two years of their arrival, the Spanish had reduced the Aztec capital from a city of unprecedented wealth and power to a pile of rubble.

COLONIAL-ERA MEXICO

Following the defeat of the Aztecs, the Spanish quickly gained control of more land; within three years, they had subjugated most of present-day Mexico, which was renamed "New Spain". Over the course of the 16th and 17th centuries, the Spanish seized Indigenous land, imposed taxes and local forms of government, and brought in missionaries from Spain to convert Indigenous people to Catholicism. They also brought new diseases, such as smallpox and measles, leading to tens of thousands of deaths.

By exploiting Mexico's natural resources, the colonial economy grew. During this time, New Spain relied heavily upon the free labour of enslaved African peoples, who were forced to work in the mines and on plantations. At the same time, new social groups were developed, largely based on skin colour. Individuals of European ancestry – known as Creoles – sat at the top of the social order, establishing haciendas for ranching and harvesting, and building grand residences and churches. Mestizos – those of mixed European and Indigenous descent – took on skilled occupations as traders, artisans and local officials, while Indigenous peoples were pushed further into the margins.

MEXICAN INDEPENDENCE

Being so geographically distant from Spain allowed Mexico partial autonomy, with its new elite growing rich and powerful. However, in the 18th century, Spain's Bourbon dynasty sought to take back control. Royal power was centralized, weakening the Church,

and relations between Spain and Mexico took a turn for the worse.

Tensions rose to breaking point on 16 September 1810, when Miguel Hidalgo (*p212*) gave his *El Grito de Dolores* ("The Cry of Dolores"), calling on his parishioners to fight for independence, though the rebellion was crushed. Another revolt in 1814, led by priest José María Morelos, was also crushed. Finally, in 1821, the Creole elite, taking advantage of the fact that Spain was distracted by the Napoleonic Wars, declared independence from the Spanish Empire. Modern Mexico was born.

A NEW NATION

After a brief imperial interlude, Mexico became a republic. The new nation was divided between Liberals, who favoured a progressive, secular and free-trading society, and Conservatives, who wanted a centralized state supported by the army and Church.

When the Liberals came to power in 1855 led by Benito Juárez, a period of sweeping social and political reforms known as *La Reforma* (The Reform) were instigated. These would separate Church and State, reduce the power of the Church, place the army under civilian control and institute a bill of rights for all citizens. The Church and the army resisted, but in the ensuing War of the Reform (1857–60) the Liberals were victorious.

Yet the conflict was far from over. In 1864 the Conservatives retaliated,

Above A mural of Pancho Villa and Emiliano Zapata by Bruno Mariscal

seeking support from Napoleon III and declaring Maximilian of Habsburg the new emperor of Mexico. It was a short-lived period of rule, however, with Maximilian executed in 1867 and the republic restored under Juárez.

THE REVOLUTION

Following Juárez's death, general Porfirio Díaz took control in 1876, instituting a three-decades-long dictatorship. Under his rule, cities grew and communications improved, but rural workers also became impoverished and Mexico's middle classes grew frustrated with an authoritarian government.

The Mexican Revolution began in 1910, instigated by disenfranchised workers furious with the rule of Díaz. The years of the revolution were marked by country-wide conflict, with revolutionary leaders Emiliano Zapata and Pancho Villa eventually defeating the ruling regime, only for the country to succumb to further violence between other revolutionary groups.

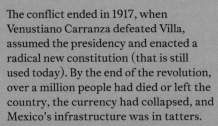

turning a domestic struggle into a heavily militarized drug war that continues to this day.

The conflict ended in 1917, when Venustiano Carranza defeated Villa, assumed the presidency and enacted a radical new constitution (that is still used today). By the end of the revolution, over a million people had died or left the country, the currency had collapsed, and Mexico's infrastructure was in tatters.

To escape from the shadow of conflict, a concerted attempt was made in the mid-20th century to create a sense of national identity that blended both Indigenous and Spanish heritage. Up until this point, Mexico's Indigenous population were still largely sidelined, but cultural projects like the Muralist Movement (p162) sought to celebrate Mexico's Indigenous heritage, creating a new image of a modern nation rising from the ashes.

RISE OF THE CARTELS

Efforts to bring about lasting peace in Mexico were thwarted by escalating struggles along the US border. Though drugs and guns had been trafficked from South America to the US via Mexico throughout the 20th century, the problem came to a head in the late 1980s. Mexico's cartels had grown in power, partly due to corrupt government officials accepting bribes, and partly due to their often violent influence in border cities like Tijuana (p32). The collapse of Colombia's powerful Cali cartel in the late 1990s left a power vacuum at the top of the drug trade, allowing Mexico's drug barons to take charge of the region's cocaine routes. Their newfound power brought about significant tensions between the cartels, local governments and the state,

LOOKING AHEAD

The early 21st century has remained turbulent for Mexico: the distribution of wealth remains imbalanced and gang violence, the influence of the cartels and migration are concerns.

However, Mexico has weathered many crises, and the future shows signs of brightness. As an export-oriented economy, Mexico relies on trade deals with the US, and strong trade has led to the country's economy becoming the world's 11th largest. The left-leaning Morena party, now the country's most popular, is looking to target corruption, while social justice movements continue to give voice to the marginalized.

Mexico's Drug War

The Mexican drug war is an ongoing conflict between the government and various drug cartels. It was in 2006 that the conflict began in earnest, when then-president Felipe Calderón launched a deadly attack, sending the military into the coastal state of Michoacán. Since then, tens of thousands of soldiers have been deployed in cities across the country (with significant funding from the US). It's estimated that more than 200,000 Mexicans – including politicians, students and journalists – have been killed in the crossfire, with thousands more "disappeared".

LEGEND *of* LA MALINCHE

La Malinche is one of the most controversial figures in Mexican history. Remembered as conquistador Hernán Cortés's translator, she worked closely with him as he conquered the Aztec Empire. Born as Malinalli in around 1500 to an Aztec family, La Malinche was sold into slavery at a young age and grew up among the Mayans. She was gifted to Cortés along with 19 other enslaved women in 1519. Given that Cortés's translator only spoke Yucatec, La Malinche proved useful by translating from the Aztec Nahuatl language into Yucatec; she soon picked up Spanish and became the conquistador's sole translator and political advisor. Following the collapse of the Aztec Empire, she gave birth to Cortés's son, Mexico's first legally recognized mestizo *(p38)*.

In the centuries since her death, La Malinche's legend has grown. To some, she's guilty of treason, of betraying her own people by helping Cortés to overthrow the Aztec Empire. To this day, the derogatory term *malinchismo* is used to denote an attraction to other cultures and a disdain for one's own. To others, she's the mother of Mexico's mestizo races, a woman who rose through the ranks to become an intermediary between cultures. Some even say the conquest would have been bloodier without her involvement.

In the 1960s, feminist movements began to reclaim the image of La Malinche. They viewed her as a scapegoat, seeing her persecution as a consequence of a misogynistic society. Whether she's seen as a victim of circumstance, a grand betrayer or a figurehead of modern Mexico, there's no denying the power of her legend.

social
Mexico

Mexico's society is as richly diverse as its geography. The country's large Indigenous population is made up of many different groups – including the descendants of the Aztecs and Mayans – each with their own distinct traditions, languages and spiritual beliefs. Over time, Spanish, African and other cultures from around the world have been woven into the country's fabric, creating a multicultural society that's unique to Mexico. And the backbone of this society? For most Mexicans, it's family. Indeed, strong familial relationships – often intertwined with equally strong Catholic beliefs – lie at the country's core, providing a sense of community and support in both good times and bad.

Mexico's Peoples

The heart of Mexico is its people. Here, Indigenous groups uphold rich traditions, those of Spanish-Indigenous ancestry celebrate their diverse heritage and global communities weave their cultures into Mexico's tapestry.

Multicultural Mexico is home to many communities, including Indigenous peoples such as the Mixtec, Zapotec and Nahuas, who have lived here for millennia. Today, many Mexicans have a mix of Indigenous, Spanish and African heritage, and refer to themselves as mestizos. But the country has also seen several other groups arrive on its shores, including Arab, Jewish and Chinese communities.

INDIGENOUS MEXICO

Descended from the first people to inhabit North America millennia ago, Mexico's Indigenous groups each have their own culture and language (p55). There were once hundreds of different Indigenous communities in Mexico, but the conflict and disease brought by the arrival of the Spanish, plus subsequent structural discrimination, has greatly reduced their numbers (p38), with just under 70 groups surviving today. Despite this, Mexico is home to the largest population of Indigenous people in North America, with over 25 million individuals calling the country home.

These communities mainly live in the south of the country: the states of Chiapas and Oaxaca, for instance, have large groups of Mixtec and Zapotec peoples, while the more rural parts of

The Impact of Development

Development in Mexico has sometimes come at the expense of the country's Indigenous people, who have lost land, access to natural resources and sacred pieces of history in Mexico's effort to modernize. One such example is the continuing rapid, and largely unchecked, development of Tulum on Mexico's Yucatán Peninsula. An increased demand for high-end property in this popular beach town led, in 2022, to the eviction of 12,000 Indigenous people from their homes.

Right A member of Mexico's Indigenous Zapotec community in the village of Santa Ana del Valle, Oaxaca

the Yucatán Peninsula are home to Maya-speaking communities (the area was once a key part of the Mayan civilization). Other groups, including the Otomi, Totonac, Tzotzil, Huastec and Nahuas, live across Mexico. The Nahuas are Mexico's largest Indigenous group, with major communities found in the Sierra Norte de Puebla, the Central Highlands and the Gulf Coast.

Many Indigenous communities continue to honour the heritage and traditions of their forebears, whether by wearing *huipils* (everyday, hand-woven dresses), engaging in agricultural economies, practising polytheistic religions or speaking Indigenous languages. The Totonac, for example, have preserved their language and many of their traditional customs, including the dance of the Voladores *(p72)*. Other groups showcase their heritage through age-old crafts, such as the fine jewellery produced by the Mixtec people or the textiles created by Zapotec communities.

FACING CHALLENGES

For Indigenous peoples in Mexico, there's often pressure to conform, whether by wearing more Western clothing, actively practising Catholicism or speaking Spanish at the expense of their own languages. In the 1990s, the emergence of the Zapatista National Liberation Army provided a platform to talk about Indigenous rights, but change has been slow to come, with Indigenous – largely rural – communities often struggling with issues such as poverty and access to education and healthcare *(p24)*.

Positively, in 2011, the Mexican Constitution was amended to state that international human rights treaties were now part of Mexican law, with the result that Indigenous communities gained the

right to campaign against injustices. This has allowed Indigenous groups such as the Choreachi to win court battles regarding ownership rights over their traditional lands – a major milestone for Indigenous rights.

MESTIZOS

Meaning "mixed person", mestizos – those of both Indigenous and European ancestry – make up the majority of the population in Mexico. Historically, members of this group held Catholic beliefs and took on skilled occupations *(p38)*, but faced prejudice because of their Indigenous heritage and were restricted from climbing higher in society.

Following the Mexican Revolution *(p40)* attitudes changed. In an attempt to create a unified Mexican nationality, those in power began to celebrate both the Indigenous and European aspects of Mexican heritage. Partly achieved via the concept of *Indigenismo*, which celebrated the role of Indigenous people in Mexico's

Above Santa María de la Ribera, an example of Arab-influenced architecture in Mexico

Left A Totonac man wearing the costume of the Voladores

which focused on the influence of Afro-Mexicans to Mexico's history, culture and modern-day society. Following this in 2015, Black was at last added as an identity option on a preliminary national census, officially recognizing those of African descent for the first time.

MULTICULTURAL MEXICO

Different immigrant communities have influenced the country's culture, among them Arabs from modern-day Lebanon and Syria. This group arrived in the port cities of Veracruz, Tampico and Progreso in the 19th and 20th centuries, in search of religious freedom and economic opportunity. Although a minority, this community has had a major impact on Mexico, including its architecture, with Moorish aesthetics visible in buildings like the Santa Maria de la Ribera.

The same period saw many Chinese immigrants arrive in the country as labourers, settling in the likes of Mexicali in Baja California; the town's cuisine, crafts and celebrations have all been influenced by this group, with a Chinese New Year Festival held annually. Today, this community continues to grow, partly thanks to Chinese companies setting up shop in cities like Ciudad Juárez.

Mexican culture has also been enriched by its Jewish community. Jews from the Middle East arrived in the 19th century, and were followed during World War II by Ashkenazi Jews from Eastern Europe, many of whom moved to Mexico City. An estimated 40,000 Jews live in Mexico; in the capital, you'll find Jewish restaurants selling Judío-Mexicano fusions, such as lox sandwiches garnished with avocado and *pico de gallo*.

history and heritage, the idea spread quickly, especially among young artists. Mexican muralists in particular began incorporating Mesoamerican figures, stories and events into their work *(p162)*. However, despite this cultural shift, the wealthiest echelons of Mexican society continued to be dominated by lighter-skinned Mexicans – a bias that is still found today.

THE THIRD ROOT

Around 2 per cent of Mexicans belong to the Afro-Mexican community, whose heritage stretches back to the colonial era *(p38)*. Concentrated in and around the states of Guerrero, Veracruz and Oaxaca, this group long struggled for recognition, despite having contributed greatly to the country, including during the Mexican Revolution, when a battalion of Afro-Mexicans fought with Emiliano Zapata. Afro-Mexicans have enriched Mexico's culture via music and dance, too: *la bamba*, a traditional Mexican song, has African roots, as does the folkloric *danza de los diablos* (Dance of the Devils) performed during the Day of the Dead.

It wasn't until 1992 that the Mexican government first began recognizing this contribution via the Third Root Project,

INDiGENOUS STORIES

Throughout history, Mexico's Indigenous peoples have created myths and legends to make sense of the world and their place within it. Mexico is enriched by these stories, which remain integral to Indigenous identities.

Myths and stories help Mexico's Indigenous communities understand the origins of the cosmos, the rhythms of nature and the changing tides of history. These myths comprise a complex belief system, describing a pantheon of deities and venerated figures, but are also used to impart time-honoured daily wisdom. Many of Mexico's Indigenous peoples relied on oral storytelling, with tales passed from generation to generation by revered storytellers.

SHARED STORIES

As Mexico's origin stories have been passed down and translated across centuries and civilizations, they have been altered, reframed and forged anew. This means the stories told today are amalgamations of many older tales, with an ever-revolving cast of animals, gods and figures. Little is conclusively known about the earliest myths of the Olmec people, for example, but jaguars and serpents featured prominently in Olmec iconography. Later Meso-american civilizations reinvented these icons, with the Aztecs worshipping a feathered serpent called Quetzalcoatl, a god who featured heavily in their own origin stories.

Stories have changed and evolved as a result of conquest and invasion, with old gods subsumed within the folklore of conquering civilizations. As the Aztec

Above A Mayan depiction of man created from corn

Left A vessel depicting a venerated Mayan maize god

Empire spread further south into Mayan territories, their gods were passed on, with Quetzalcoatl becoming Kukulkan to the Mayans. Dramatic floods also feature prominently in Indigenous stories, with Indigenous flood myths predating the arrival of the Bible with its own flood story.

TALES OF CORN

As central to Mesoamerican folklore as it has been to diets, corn features heavily in the region's mythology. The Mayans worshipped a maize god, and told of humans made from corn. The first part of the Popol Vuh, the sacred text that contains the history of the K'iche' people (a civilization of Mayan origin

Above Dancers hold
a representation of
the god Quetzalcoatl

Above right Moon
over the desert;
the Aztecs saw a
rabbit's reflection

that rose in what is now Guatemala)
written in 1505, describes how the
K'iche' came into existence. Tepeu, the
god of the skies, and Gucamatz, the god
of the seas, created humans after three
attempts, only succeeding when they
added yellow corn to form flesh and
red corn to form blood.

According to the legend of the
Rarámuri people, in the beginning of the
world, the Sun and the Moon were small
children dressed in maguey leaves, living
alone in a small house. Onorúame, the
sun god, sought to give them company,
so he husked several ears of corn to form
a man, blowing on him three times to

give him life. Then he created a woman,
blowing four times to ensure she had the
additional strength to birth children.
Today, the first Rarámuri couple are
symbolized by the two-ended ribbon
that men wear on their heads: one end
represents the woman and the other
end the man.

NATURAL CONNECTIONS
Stories weren't only used to explain
human origins, but also to forge connections with the natural world. The
Aztecs, for example, believed there was
a silhouette of a rabbit on the moon.
Legend described how Quetzalcoatl

villages. The shaman enlisted the help of the rain god, Yuku, before turning to the obedient toad Bobok, who masterminded a plan to bring rain back to the parched land.

CONTEMPORARY STORYTELLING

These myths and thousands like them continue to circulate to this day, fostering connections between communities and tying modern Indigenous peoples to their ancestors.

The Wixáritari (or Huichol) are a small group living in western Mexico in the Sierra Madre Occidental Mountains. They have maintained many of their storytelling traditions, and are relatively unique in that their stories remain uninfluenced by Catholic theology. In their rural home, they still have ceremonies celebrating the seasons, with shaman using stories to bring *"kupuri"*, or life force, into the souls of the people.

These stories also have an important political role that can be traced back to the Spanish conquest. To centralize and strengthen European narratives, the Spanish suppressed Indigenous writing systems and destroyed written testimony. In the face of this destruction, oral tales were a key means of preserving the past and sharing wisdom. Indigenous groups are still using storytelling to reclaim histories, refute colonial narratives and draw attention to environmental issues. Teaching stories is key to Indigenous education, with grassroots efforts in states like Oaxaca ensuring young people are aware of their heritage. Encoded in these stories is centuries of hard-won wisdom that can still guide through the complexities of the modern world.

descended to Earth in human form to explore the world he helped create. As he wandered through the Anáhuac, the heartland of Aztec Mexico, he soon fell ravenously hungry. One evening, a rabbit offered Quetzalcoatl grass to eat, but the god refused, claiming he did not eat grass. The rabbit then offered himself as food for Quetzalcoatl so he could regain his strength. Moved, Quetzalcoatl took the rabbit on a journey to get a closer look at the moon; upon the rabbit's return to earth, its reflection remained imprinted on the moon, a final gift from Quetzalcoatl for the creature's unprompted generosity.

Other Indigenous groups also use myths to understand natural phenomena. To explain the origin of rain, the Yaqui people of Sonora believe that a severe drought brought extreme thirst to their

LANGUAGES

Spanish might be the most common language in Mexico, but the country nevertheless contains rich linguistic variety, with distinct regional languages spoken by many Indigenous groups.

Spanish is one of the world's most spoken languages, with roughly 500 million people speaking it. A good chunk of them are in Mexico, the largest Spanish-speaking country in the world – although one that puts its own spin on the mother tongue.

MEXICAN SPANISH

For Mexico's Indigenous peoples, Spanish was first encountered as the language of the conquistadors. Today, the Mexican version is a vibrant composite of regional influences, with five broad dialects: Baja Californian, Northern, Central, Coastal and Southern. And while the language comes from Europe, Mexican Spanish differs starkly from that spoken in Spain.

One way this difference can be felt is in pronunciation – in Spain, for example, *gracias* is mostly pronounced *"grathias"*, while in Mexico it's the more phonetic *"grasias"*. A European Spanish speaker

Above A sign in Spanish above a store in Cuetzalan, Puebla, stating, "Passion fruit ice pops for sale"

visiting Mexico would likely also be perplexed by the suite of slang phrases in everyday speech ("*¡A huevo!*" in Mexico has little to do with eggs, instead meaning something close to "Hell yeah!").

THE ALBUR

The differences don't end there. Combine the playful streak of Mexican slang with a Catholic-infused embarrassment when it comes to sex, and you get the *albur*, or double entendre. There are few phrases in Mexico that can't be loaded with sexual double meaning; those unfamiliar with Mexican conversation may be surprised by the frequent stifled laughter from their friends (*albur* is seen as inappropriate among families). Objects with phallic characteristics, such as chillis, are often used to craft double entendres – bringing a whole new meaning to the phrase *"Te gusta el chile?"* ("Do you like chilli?"). Some suggest this wordplay originated as a form of entertainment in the mines of central Mexico, while others believe its roots run to Indigenous peoples subverting a language imposed upon them. Either way, the *albur* is a reminder of Mexico's inventive linguistic traditions.

INDIGENOUS LANGUAGES

Despite its dominance, Spanish is a relatively modern language in Mexico. Before it arrived in the 16th century, different Indigenous groups conversed using around 500 languages; now, that number lies at around 280, with roughly 8 million people speaking one or more of these Indigenous languages, many as native speakers. The most common languages are Nahuatl, whose 1.4 million speakers live around Veracruz, Hidalgo and Puebla; Yucatecan Maya, hailing from the Yucatán Peninsula, with around 750,000 speakers; and Mixteco in the southwest, with half a million speakers. But these languages are at risk. Around 60 per cent are predicted to disappear within the next century, with the likes of Ayapaneco in Tabasco now understood by just a handful of people. This is in part due to decades of discriminatory attitudes and policies, which forbade the teaching of non-Spanish languages in schools, and in part due to the effects of migration; younger speakers are increasingly motivated to learn English as a way to secure a better life in places like the US.

Since the early 2000s, attempts have been made to prevent this loss. In 2003, the General Law of Indigenous Peoples' Linguistic Rights was approved. This law recognizes 68 Indigenous languages as official, naming them national languages due to their historical origin. Such efforts are crucial, as languages are about more than communication: after all, they hold beliefs, histories and identities.

Grassroots Preservation

As well as government efforts, several grassroots attempts have been made to preserve Indigenous languages, including local speakers compiling dictionaries, creating apps and even offering free classes. Creative content is also becoming more readily available, including poetry collections compiled in writers' mother tongues, such as those by Mikeas Sánchez (a Zoque speaker), or the animated Indigenous stories of 68 Voices, 68 Hearts, each of which is narrated in an Indigenous language.

Spoken in **Baja California**, Kiliwa (or Koleeu ñaja') is part of the Yuman language branch and is among the most endangered of Mexico's languages. Though Kiliwa is rarely written, a Spanish-Kiliwa dictionary was published in 2006.

ON THE MAP

INDIGENOUS LANGUAGES

Around 6 per cent of the Mexican population speak an Indigenous language, with over 250 different languages found across the country. Some of these languages are spoken by hundreds of thousands of people, while others are in use by only a handful. Here is a small snapshot of the Indigenous linguistic variety on offer in Mexico.

Among the few Indigenous languages in Mexico with no direct ties to existing language groups, Seri (or Cmiique iitom) is considered a language isolate. It is spoken by fewer than 1,000 people in just two remote villages in the state of **Sonora**: Desemboque and Punta Chueca.

Spoken by 140,000 people in **Oaxaca**, Mixe (or Ayuujk) encompasses at least six distinct variants. But learners are welcome; Mixe has its own dedicated language learning app, Kumoontun, and is broadcast on Indigenous radio station XEGLO.

Critically endangered, Ayapenaco in **Tabasco** is spoken by fewer than two dozen people. There are ongoing efforts to revive it, including free classes offered to young people in Jalpa de Méndez, Tabasco.

Spoken in the state of **Chiapas**, Tsotsil (also known as Tzotzil or Bats'i k'op) is one of Mexico's most interesting regional languages. Not only are there several rock bands who sing in Tsotsil, including Yibel, Sak Tzevul *(pictured)* and Vayijel, it's one of the few Indigenous languages to see a recent uptick in speakers.

One of the officially recognized languages of Mexico, Totonac actually encompasses several distinct but related variants and dialects, including Papantlá Totonac and Yecuatla Totonac. Today, it's spoken by around 200,000 people, including many in **Veracruz**. There are also speakers found in neighbouring Puebla and Hidalgo.

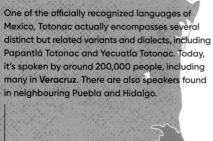

Family Ties

Family is the bedrock of Mexican society, with parents, siblings, grandparents, cousins, aunts and uncles all playing a role. And though domestic structures are ever-evolving, one thing remains true: family comes first.

In Mexico and much of Latin America, a great deal of importance is placed on *familismo*, or dedication to family. Regularly spending time together, seeking and giving advice on both the big and little things, and offering care in times of hardship are part and parcel of daily life.

THE FAMILY UNIT

Until the early 20th century, a typical Mexican family consisted of a mother, father and between 10 and 15 children. Such a large number of kids was in part due to Catholic beliefs, which encouraged married couples to procreate. Extended family units were also common, particularly in rural areas, with grandparents, aunts, uncles and cousins all living in the same households or neighbourhoods. This tapestry of intergenerational connection bears close relation to historic Mesoamerican family structures. In Aztec society, for example, families often lived in close quarters, with children collectively raised by numerous female members of a community.

As it did around the world, urbanization made its impact on Mexican society, with higher costs of living and smaller homes leading to smaller families. The close-knit element of family life continues to thrive, however, thanks partly to the strong support system it offers – a crucial benefit in a country that has traditionally lacked access to social services.

FAMILIAL ROLES

Traditionally, there have been strict role divisions within Mexican families. This links back to Mesoamerican and Catholic family structures, both of which were patriarchal and reinforced rigid gender roles. To this day, families are generally dominated by the father, who is seen as the undisputed *jefe de familia* (head of the household). He is the family's breadwinner and protector, as well as the one who imposes family discipline. Such roles are inextricably tied to the idea of machismo, where men are expected to be strong, self-reliant and dominant individuals, and to downplay any feelings of compassion or sentiment, which are often regarded as more feminine qualities.

Above right A grandfather and his grandchildren

Right Preparing breakfast in Oaxaca

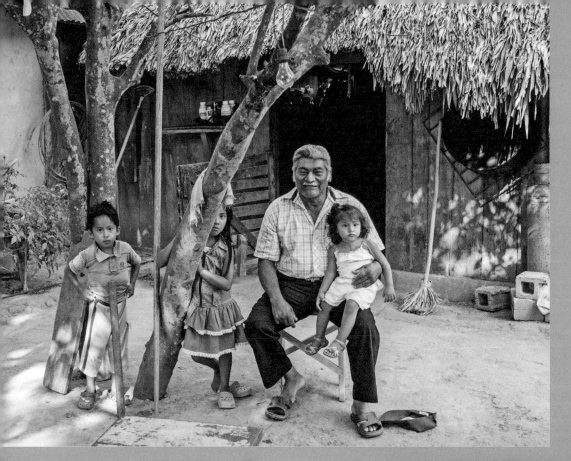

Women, on the other hand, are held to the idea of Marianismo, which links back to Catholic ideals of the Virgin Mary. This concept sees women as submissive and self-sacrificing, especially when it comes to family. It's no surprise, then, that in most Mexican families the mother is traditionally in charge of domestic duties such as cooking, cleaning and child-rearing. Although this maternal role restricts women's independence – both socially and economically – it also comes with immense power. A mother's duties are integral to the proper functioning of the household, and most Mexicans still give much respect to their mother and their *abuela* (grandmother), both of whom are seen as formidable figures.

STORIES FROM MEXICO

I grew up in a family of six, made up of myself, my parents and my three siblings. My siblings and I used to play all the time, especially my younger brother and me – he's only two years younger than me. My oldest brother and my sister are named after my parents. They have the exact-same name. I was the first one to have my own name, and I think that gave me a little bit more of an independent identity.

We all went to the same school. It was a Catholic school where my mom was also a teacher. My dad, meanwhile, worked at a petrochemical company and as we were growing up we only saw him at night. We used to visit my *abuela* every weekend. She was almost 100 years old, and she lived three hours away from our house. During my college years I would spend my entire vacation time with her. She loved my poetry and she would always give me advice on my life and relationships.

Carlos José Pérez Sámano,
Colorado, US

FAMILY VALUES

And it's not just *abuela*. Elders in general are held in high regard. As the holders of ancestral wisdom, their life experiences are treated with reverence. Older relatives often take on advisory roles within the family, with younger members consulting them on all manner of issues. In today's multigenerational families, many grandparents and older relatives also take an active part in raising kids. This caregiving relationship is later reciprocated; it remains an entrenched custom here to care for older family members rather than outsourcing this responsibility to a care home. This is partly due to the strong bonds that exist between family members, but also partly due to a lack of state-provided or affordable care options.

Above Generations of a family in Oaxaca
Right A family watching a parade pass by their home

Cost concerns also lead some families to adopt a more frugal approach to living; clothes and toys are often handed down from older to younger siblings, for example, although this desire is also linked to family values of sharing. This also extends to the notion of inheritance: keeping property within the family is seen as important; as such, the country has no inheritance tax.

Another abiding family value is the importance of spending time together. In many Mexican families, for example, Sunday remains family time. Even for those who no longer see family at church, the last day of the week is reserved for large family gatherings. The *sobremesa* *(p94)* is often an important part of these meet-ups, with family members catching up on each other's lives and asking for advice if needed. It's also a time when important family decisions will be made.

CHANGING DYNAMICS

As time marches on, Mexico's family units are ever evolving. Global migration, increased access to education and job opportunities mean families are sometimes separated by distance. More women are entering the workforce and a greater number of men are taking on domestic duties. Having a family, for some, is being deferred, largely down to living costs and limited housing. Others are choosing to live outside of traditional family structures, including cohabiting couples, LGBTQ+ families and those remarrying after divorce.

Yet, while families may look different in the 21st century, the strength of the family unit itself survives, much as it has done for centuries. What makes a family might be changing, but one thing's for certain: the importance of family to Mexican society is going nowhere.

HOME REMEDIES

Whenever someone is feeling a little under the weather in Mexico, they'll usually turn to their *abuela*. After all, Mexican grandmothers are known for their ability to rustle up effective home remedies at the drop of a hat. Many of the treatments they sternly advocate for have been handed down through the generations, passed from grandmother to daughter to granddaughter. Most are also cheap and easy to whip up, being made from a handful of ingredients, often purchased from the local market.

Remedies are available for a myriad of mild health issues, from using aloe vera to help with cuts and burns to drinking an infusion of bougainvillea flower with honey and lime to fend off the flu. They're not just old wives' tales, either; many of these panaceas have a medical element. For instance, a piece of raw potato blended with water is given to someone with gastritis, as the starch within the plant can help counteract any acidity in the stomach.

While some of these remedies are more modern, such as rubbing *vaporu* (also known as VapoRub) on your neck and chest when you have a cough, many have their roots in ancient Indigenous medicinal knowledge. The Aztecs, for instance, had a deep understanding of the healing properties of many plants, something shown in the *Codex de la Cruz-Badiano*. Written by an Aztec healer in the 16th century, this illustrated manuscript details a wealth of Indigenous herbal treatments. Some of this ancestral know-how has been carried forward into home remedies today, making one thing for certain – *abuela* knows best.

Religion and Spirituality

Bringing Mexicans together, religion and spirituality is at the core of daily life. In many places, Catholic beliefs have become intertwined with Indigenous ones, leading to a religious syncretism that's unique to Mexico.

Mexico is a decidedly Catholic country, with over 80 per cent of the population considering themselves followers of the faith. Rich Catholic symbolism and ritual form the basis of religious activity here, with major life events marked by the church and reverent festivals a regular occurance. Yet Mexican Catholicism has been heavily influenced by and blended with Indigenous spirituality, whose roots can be traced back to mighty Mesoamerican gods and beyond.

MESOAMERICAN BELIEFS

While Mesoamerican civilizations such as the Olmecs, Mayans and Aztecs (p36) each possessed their own unique rituals and practices, they also had similarities. All were polytheistic systems that worshipped a pantheon of gods, many of whom were linked to the natural world. For the Aztecs, two of the most important gods were Huitzilopochtli, the god of the sun (and of war), who was depicted as either a hummingbird or an eagle, and Tlaloc, the god of rain, water and earthly fertility. Their importance was underpinned by the fact that both agriculture and war were central parts of the Aztecs' culture and economy. Mayan gods were linked to natural phenomena, too, with diffe-rent deities for things like fire, lightning and wind.

A SENSE OF SACRIFICE

The role of priests was of the utmost importance in many of these societies, with these individuals usually holding high-ranking positions. As well as being scholars, astronomers and diviners, they provided a link between the people and the gods, and were responsible for per-forming rituals to appease the latter. Often, this would involve sacrifice, some-thing believed to be necessary to ensure general societal well-being. According to these groups, blood contained a powerful life force that could invoke the gods' blessings. The Aztecs, for instance, under-took ritual sacrifice as a way to make sure that the sun would continue to rise and that crops would keep growing.

Sacrifice ranged from incense burning and food offerings to gorier acts, such as removing the hearts of living humans.

Right A modern-day healer performing a ritual in Mexico City

MAYAN GODS

Itzamna
The most important of the Mayan deities, Itzamna was the god of fire who created the earth and who ruled over heaven.

Kukulkan
This feathered serpent god, often depicted as a dragon, was believed to be a creator responsible for bringing rain and wind.

Bolon Tzacab
Mayan rulers often held a sceptre in the form of this leaf-nosed god, who is linked to agriculture.

Chaac
This god was depicted with a lightning axe, which he used to strike the clouds to make storms.

For the Aztecs, war on neighbouring groups provided captives whose blood purified new temples and empowered gods such as Huitzilopochtli. However, it was acts of self-sacrifice, such as fasting and blood-letting, that were the most common rituals. Powerful Mayan rulers publicly practised such rituals, including piercing their tongues or genitalia; these were striking displays of courage and devotion to the nation's welfare.

ADVENT OF CATHOLICISM

When the Spanish first arrived in Mexico in the 16th century, they brought with them a fervent belief in Catholicism and a desire to spread their faith. Forced conversions and religious violence during the Spanish era defined the early days of the religion in Mexico, but now the Catholic church knits the nation together. This is partly due to the fact that, over time, Indigenous beliefs have become woven into the Catholic faith. And nowhere is this better seen than in the country's patron saint, the Virgin of Guadalupe.

According to legend, this image of a brown-skinned Virgin Mary appeared in 1531 to Juan Diego, an Indigenous man and a Christian convert. Diego saw the miraculous figure as he was passing Tepeyac, the hilltop site the Aztecs believed to belong to the Aztec mother goddess Tonantzin. He appealed to the local Catholic bishop to build a shrine in that location, but the latter was unwilling. Afterwards, the Virgin appeared to Juan Diego again and told him to bring the bishop flowers from the hill as proof. When Juan Diego returned with the blooms in his cape, the image of the Virgin appeared on the garment, convincing the bishop to establish the Basílica de Santa María de Guadalupe

(*p68*). The fact that the apparition of Mary resembled the Indigenous population and that the site she appeared at had Aztec heritage meant the event struck a chord with the local people, and was crucial in helping Catholicism take root in Mexico. Although some now regard this event with suspicion, there's no denying the reverence held for the Virgin of Guadalupe across the country: for many, she's revered for her ties to Indigenous spirituality and is regarded as the mother of all Mexicans.

BLENDING OF BELIEFS

Today, Catholicism is regarded as the predominant religion in Mexico, and for many Mexicans, Catholic rituals and practices are an intrinsic part of everyday life. Believers exercise their faith by attending weekly mass and keeping

Above A church filled with worshippers

Left Depiction of the Virgin of Guadalupe

altars with images of saints in their homes. Major life events are tied to the church, too, from baptism and first communion to confirmation and marriage, and the faithful mark the months of the year by an ongoing cycle of Catholic feasts and fiestas, including Semana Santa and Corpus Christi.

Yet Indigenous spiritual beliefs have their place. Many lifelong Catholics, for instance, have a healthy respect for Indigenous nature spirits. These include *ehecame* (winds), which are believed to afflict the nervous system, and *nahuales*, personal guardian spirits that exist as counterparts to human souls. When dealing with sickness, it's common to couple prayers to a Catholic saint with a visit to a local curandero (traditional healer). These respected individuals – who approach healing from the Indigenous understanding that ailments have both a spiritual cause and a cure – will use everything from incense and herbs to ritual baths and animal sacrifice (such as a chicken) to restore their patients' health.

The fusion of these belief systems reaches a pinnacle each year during Día de los Muertos *(p190)*, where mostly Catholic celebrants offer food to their dead ancestors. During this event, Christian ideologies of eternal heaven and hell sit alongside older Indigenous perspectives of a more cyclical view of life and death. It's one of many examples of how religion in Mexico blends Catholic and Indigenous beliefs, helping to weave a colourful tapestry of spiritual life.

CHURCHES

Countless churches dot Mexico, emblems of the population's strong Catholic faith. Many of these churches, however, are fused with markers of Indigenous belief: a glimpse of a historic pyramid peaking out beneath a church; nature-inspired carvings decorating church interiors; or Mayan rituals continuing to take place in hallowed halls.

IGLESIA DE SAN JUAN PARANGARICUTIRO

Back in February 1943, Parícutin – the world's youngest volcano – started oozing lava across the surrounding area. The entire village of San Parangaricutiro was consumed by the red-hot stone, but, amazingly, its church was left largely unscathed – something seen as an act of God. Even though lava rock eventually buried most of the church over the next year or so, it never touched its altar or tower; the latter continues to rise above the half-consumed church, acting as a symbol of local strength and resilience.

BASÍLICA DE SANTA MARÍA DE GUADALUPE

This modern, tent-shaped basilica in Mexico City was constructed in the mid-1970s to replace a much-loved older basilica of the same name, whose structural integrity had been affected by subsidence and earthquakes. It houses one of Mexico's most holy items: a 500-year-old *tilma* (cloak) marked with the image of the Virgin of Guadalupe *(p66)* and believed to be a manifestation of the saint. Each year upwards of 20 million people pilgrimage here to pay homage to the Virgin, making it one of the world's most visited churches.

IGLESIA DE NUESTRA SEÑORA DE LOS REMEDIOS

Watched over by Popocatépetl, this yellow church in Puebla was built by the Spanish in the 16th century on top of the Aztecs' Tlachihualtepetl, a huge pyramid. Apart from its eye-catching hue, the Neo-Classical church dazzles with its intricate Talavera tiles and gilded vaults.

IGLESIA DE SAN JUAN CHAMULA

Chiapas is famous for its fierce resistance to colonial, Catholic and government influence. It's unsurprising, then, that this Mexican state is home to a church known more for its Indigenous rites than its Catholic rituals. There's no pews or priest here; instead, worshippers sit among pine needles scattered on the floor and light multicoloured candles, while curanderos perform traditional Mayan rituals in the local Tzotzil language. It's a powerful example of thriving Indigenous beliefs.

IGLESIA DE SANTA MARÍA DE TONANTZINTLA

This church in Cholula beautifully showcases Mexico's religious syncretism. It was erected by Franciscan monks in the late 1700s, who partnered with local Indigenous artists to design and decorate the church. The result is a blend of Indigenous and European styles *(p160)*, with every inch of the sanctuary's walls decorated with things like local flowers, native birds, and regional fruits and vegetables, as well as angels and cherubs.

1 Iglesia de San Juan Parangaricutiro in Michoacán

2 The blue roof of the Basílica de Santa María de Guadalupe, with the older church in front

3 Iglesia de Nuestra Señora de los Remedios, with Popocatépetl soaring behind the church

4 Iglesia de San Juan Chamula in Chiapas

5 Cholula's Iglesia de Santa María de Tonantzintla

ON THE MAP

INDIGENOUS RITUALS

Passed from one generation to the next, Indigenous rituals are an enduring part of Mexico's rich cultural heritage. Many traditions reinforce a collective sense of purpose, with ceremonies often involving cooperation and coordination among members of the community. This map highlights a number of Mexico's time-honoured Indigenous practices.

On 12 March, the Nahuatl-speaking people of Santiago Xalitzintla, in the state of **Puebla**, engage in a centuries-old ritual to honour the volcano Popocatépetl. The community recites prayers and presents offerings, including flowers, to the volcano, in the hope that it will extend goodwill to them and not erupt.

In September, the people of Tepoztlán in **Morelos** remember the legacy of King Tepoztécatl, the area's last *tlatoani* (ruler). The event involves a dramatic re-enactment of Tepoztécatl's baptism, his later encounter with opposing rulers and his success in convincing them to also convert to Catholicism.

Catemaco in **Veracruz** is renowned for its vibrant shamanic traditions. Here, revered healers blend ancient Indigenous practices with a mixture of Catholic rites and Afro-Mexican belief systems, such as voodoo, performing ceremonies that address physical ailments and emotional turmoil.

In the **Yucatán Peninsula** *(p11)*, many communities of Mayan descent believe in the existence of *Aluxes*, small magical beings thought to be guardians of nature. Rituals are sometimes performed to seek their consent for things like entering a cenote or sowing fields; shamans set up altars, burn incense and recite prayers.

In March, the people of Ixtaczoquitlán in **Veracruz** observe Xochitlallis, a ritual to honour Mother Earth and ask her for a good harvest. As part of the event, participants adorn an outdoor altar with sugar cane, flowers, corn, coffee, candles and beer.

Los

VOLADORES

The Totonac people in Veracruz are famous for *la danza de los Voladores* (The Dance of the Flyers), a millennia-old Mesoamerican fertility ritual. In this sacred spectacle, Los Voladores (The Flyers) climb to the top of a 30-m (100-ft) pole, each using a rope tied to their waist; once they reach the summit, they circle the pole, wrapping the ropes around it; finally, they descend headfirst from the top, spiralling downwards towards earth as their ropes unwind.

While the Totonac are generally considered keepers of this tradition, the ritual carries deep spiritual and cultural significance for Indigenous groups across Mexico and much of Central America. According to legend, the first *danza* was an urgent plea to the rain god, Xipe, during a severe drought centuries ago. Today, the fertility ritual is performed around the key agricultural periods, such as sowing and harvest times, and for cosmic events such as the solstices and equinoxes. Interestingly, in another example of Mexico's religious syncretism, it's also performed for some Catholic patron saint festivals, including the Día de la Virgen de Guadalupe *(p200)*.

The dance is awash with symbolism. The four dancers represent the elements of earth, air, fire and water, with the fifth Volador, who stays sitting atop the pole throughout the performance, regarded as the sun. The dancers also make 52 circuits around the pole as they descend, an act that represents the number of years found within a Mayan Great Year. Even the vibrant embroidered clothing and ornate headdresses of the dancers are symbolic: they mimic the plumage of native birds, tying back to Mayan creation stories.

Mexico
and the US

With 48 crossings on their border and a ceaseless flow of people, cultures and commodities, the US and Mexico are engaged in constant trade. Throughout their history, their fortunes have been inextricably linked.

The border between Tijuana in north-western Mexico and San Ysidro in California is often regarded as the most crossed border in the world. It has become a complex symbol of migration between Mexico and the US, with contemporary political debates prone to misrepresenting the complex and fascinating relationship between the two countries. With around 11 million living north of the border, Mexicans comprise the biggest immigrant population in the US, and their influence looms large across language, politics, food, art and architecture.

EARLY MIGRATION

The relationship between the two countries began well before the US existed in its modern form, with many US states originally a part of Mexico. Texas only became independent from Mexico in 1836, before becoming the 28th US state in 1845, while California was transferred from Mexico to the US in 1847, after the end of the Mexican–American war. Campo de Cahuenga Museum in LA's San Fernando Valley marks the spot where the declaration ending the war was signed.

In the 20th century, Mexicans began moving to the US in large numbers, influenced by political turbulence in revolutionary Mexico and a burgeoning agricultural industry in the southern US states. Following the Great Depression in the 1930s, rural migrants moved on to American cities in search of work. The move exacerbated racial struggles that would continue throughout the 20th century, with migrants facing hostility and major unemployment.

These waves of migration meant the Southwest became home to a substantial Chicano population (ie those of Mexican descent born in America). The term "chicano" was long used as a slur for Mexican immigrants, before it was reclaimed in the 1940s. It has since become a vital marker of identity and culture for Americans who embrace their Hispanic heritage; the Chicano Movement of the 1950s and 60s was a powerful antiracism campaign, focused on empowering America's Mexican peoples. Thanks in part to the efforts

Above right Crossing the border from Mexico into El Paso, Texas

STORIES FROM MEXICO

I was born in the border town of Tijuana, Mexico, and I came to the US when I was seven years old. During my first year of living in the US, my siblings, my father and I would travel to Tijuana every Friday to see my mother and four siblings who stayed behind. Despite being part of a large family with deep roots in Mexico, I felt I didn't know enough about my heritage, and there was always the curiosity to know about the country where I was born.

Fast-forward to my college years, when I went on a study-abroad programme to Mexico City. During this time I travelled solo all over Mexico as far as Veracruz and all the way to the jungle in Chiapas. I also took an all-night bus ride to the beaches of San Pancho, Nayarit to relax during spring break.

These experiences led me to realize that I was part of the country that I was born in, but also helped me to understand that I was American. I have adopted some of the mainstream values of US culture through my years of schooling and living in the US. These experiences led me to a profound realization about my dual identity.

Mónica Galván, San Diego, US

of the Chicano Movement and a broader shift in public opinion following World War II (many Mexicans fought in the war), Mexican Americans and their descendants began to be seen as a vital part of US society.

MEXICAN HEARTLANDS
Hispanic people have played a major role in US population growth, account-ing for 50 per cent of the country's growth between 2010 and 2020. Almost 60 per cent of Mexican immigrants in the US today live in the border states of California and Texas, with cities in

these states (like LA, which has the biggest population of Mexicans outside of Mexico) most visibly influenced by Mexican culture. Hundreds of thousands of people commute across the border on a daily basis, for work, to see family and friends or to attend school.

This large population means those of Mexican descent have a significant economic impact in the US. Nearly 5 million Hispanic-owned businesses contribute over $800 billion to the economy annually while employing hundreds of thousands of people. Mexico has long relied on its northern neighbour for both imports and exports, but in 2023 Mexico became America's largest trading partner, highlighting the reciprocity of their economic relations. The USMCA (the United States–Mexico–Canada Agreement) replaced NAFTA (the North American Free Trade Agreement) in 2020 in an attempt to encourage strong trade and to maintain close economic ties between Mexico and its powerful northern neighbours.

CULTURAL INFLUENCE

Aside from economics, Mexicans continue to exert a huge cultural influence across the US. But to speak of a single Mexican American culture would do a disservice to the diversity of Mexican peoples; there is a range of distinct populations and a host of cuisines, histories and communities.

In Texas, for example, the term "Tejano" refers to descendants of the first Spanish, Mexican and Indigenous families on the Texas frontier, but also to modern Texans of Mexican descent.

Their cultural influence in the state runs deep: many classics of Tex-Mex (*p100*) owe their existence to pioneering Mexican chefs in San Antonio, where those of Hispanic descent comprise 64 per cent of the population. Mexican influence in the city is also seen during public holidays: two Mexican holidays – Cinco de Mayo (5 May; *p213*) and Mexican Independence Day (16 September; *p212*) – play as big a role in civic life as the Fourth of July.

Much like San Antonio, Los Angeles has long had a thriving Mexican culture. The bustling Olvera Street in the city's historic centre, the renowned Mariachi

Above The border between Tijuana and San Ysidro

Left *Elote*, a street food as popular in LA as it is in Mexico

Plaza and the Chicano Resource Center (CRC) are meeting places for the city's Mexican communities, while the sprawling Vallarta supermarkets (first established by Mexicans in the city in the 1980s) sell a range of Latin American goods, from baked treats to tortillas and coffee.

LOOKING AHEAD

Despite the sizeable population of Mexicans and their descendants in the US, these communities remain underrepresented in state and federal politics, while divisive politicians continue to sow fear and to downplay Mexican contribution to US society. With immigration only set to rise in the coming years, cooperation will be essential to both countries' societies and economies.

Lowrider Culture

The large Mexican population of Española, New Mexico, has long expressed itself through lowrider culture. Starting in the 1940s, young Chicano communities customized cars, lowering their bodies and spray-painting them with Indigenous symbols or religious figures. The aim of lowriders is to cruise slowly, parading the vehicle's bright colours and clever modifications (including hydraulics which make the vehicles "bounce"). Today, lowriders continue to cruise through the streets as a reminder of Mexican American autonomy and pride.

Mexico's flavours have long been celebrated beyond its borders. Tacos, enchiladas and mole are found on menus around the world, while smooth-tasting tequila is a mainstay in countless bars. Yet Mexican cuisine is much more than these iconic dishes and drinks, thanks in large part to the country's abundance of ingredients. Time-honoured and carefully guarded regional recipes also play a role, and are lovingly handed down from generation to generation. It's little surprise, then, that food and drink are a celebrated part of everyday life for locals, whether it's grabbing an on-the-go *antojito* (snack) from a street-food stall or lingering with family over a home-cooked meal.

THE MEXICAN COOKBOOK

Tacos, fajitas and frijoles: these staples of Mexican cuisine are global favourites. Little wonder, then, that Mexican food is recognized by the United Nations as part of the Intangible Cultural Heritage of Humanity.

Mexican food is celebrated around the world, but what makes the country's cuisine so distinct and globally adored? Its success is rooted in solid ingredients, mixing of flavours and a healthy pinch of culinary flair.

CORN AND COUNTRY

Early Mesoamerican agriculturalists began harvesting the country's fertile soil some 12,000 years ago, producing core ingredients that would transform cuisine both inside and outside of Mexico. Foremost among these ingredients was corn, or maize. In Mexico, as the saying goes, *sin maíz, no hay país*: without corn, there is no country.

Around 3,500 years ago, Mexico's Indigenous farmers developed the

Above Farm workers harvesting corn

Above left Sunset over a cornfield in the state of Zacatecas

complex process of nixtamalization, whereby kernels of corn were cooked and soaked in an alkaline solution. The outer cover of the kernel could then be peeled off, making it much easier to grind the corn into dough, called *masa*. Whether stuffed with different vegetables or meats, boiled into what is known as a tamale, or cooked into a tortilla, *masa* is perhaps the most recognizable staple of Mexican cuisine.

KEY INGREDIENTS

Alongside corn, ancient farmers cultivated squash and beans in a practice known as the *milpa*, or "three sisters", a technique based around maximizing crop efficiency that is still used to this day. The stalk of the corn helps support the climbing bean plant, beans add nitrogen to the soil, while the squash provides shade and reduces moisture loss. This trio – corn, squash and beans – remains central to Mexican diets.

Other key ingredients grown by ancient Mexicans and still used in modern kitchens include a variety of cactus known in Mexico as *nopal* and tomatoes, which are originally from South America but were domesticated in Mexico as far back as 500 BCE. The Aztecs also grew many types of fruits

Above Making tortillas at a market in Jalisco

Above right A bean and corn seller refilling his stock in Chiapas

like guavas, papayas and mamey, a sweet avocado–like fruit with a unique reddish–pink flesh, as well as the prickly pear.

Indigenous communities would mostly grill or boil their vegetables, and, like their contemporary descendants, the ancient Aztecs liked to mix ingredients to form complex salsas and seasonings for their dishes. Many of these herbs, seeds and spices are still used in cuisines around the world, including cinnamon, coriander, avocado leaves, vanilla, cacao and, of course, many kinds of chillies.

MEAT AND PROTEIN

Mexico's abundant landscapes and pioneering techniques for growing crops meant ancient Mexican cultures tended to be largely vegetarian. The limited meat they ate was supplied by wild animals including deer, rabbit and turkey. For protein, Aztecs in the Valley of Mexico also harvested and ate a kind of crayfish called *acocil*, as well as the algae that grew in local lakes, alongside maguey worms, ants and crickets, which can still be found in the large markets of

prepared the dish using wild boar or deer, and cooked it in a *pib*, a kind of underground oven, thus the name *pibil*. These days, the meat is more commonly barbecued, but the process closely resembles that used centuries ago.

REGIONAL VARIETIES

In a country as vast as Mexico, different takes on these staple ingredients are inevitable. Mexico's diversity of crop production is due largely to its range of temperatures: Mediterranean and semi-arid in the north, temperate and sub-tropical in the centre, and tropical in the south. Like almost all ingredients in Mexico, chillies vary greatly depending on the climate, soil and topography of the region where they're grown (*p90*). As a result, the sauces they're used in also differ from one part of the country to another.

It's common to speak of nine different regional cuisines in Mexico. In the north, a strong ranching tradition has led to a heavy reliance on beef, and the region is particularly associated with grilled foods. In the coastal regions of Baja California, cuisine tends to revolve around locally caught seafood, with shrimp tacos a favourite. The Yucatán Peninsula sits between the Caribbean Sea and the Gulf of Mexico, and its location has influenced its flavours. Here, a strong Mayan tradition combined with Caribbean and Middle Eastern influences means habanero

central Mexico and Oaxaca. Today, insects can be some of the most expensive and sought-after ingredients in Mexico's markets, with *chicatanas* – large winged ants – fetching high prices, for use in a range of salsas. A new generation of chefs are incorporating insects into their menus as a means of exploring Mexico's culinary heritage.

With the arrival of the conquistadors, Mexico was introduced to pork, beef, lamb, goat and chicken, which are now ubiquitous across the country. Ancient methods still dominate, though, with techniques and flavours rooted in Indigenous cultures. A good example of this is *cochinita pibil*, a juicy pulled pork that is common in the Yucatán Peninsula. Originally, ancient Mayans

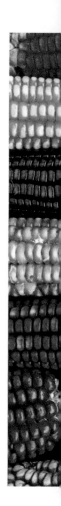

STORIES FROM MEXICO

My name is Arturo Sosa and I am a chef originally from the city of Oaxaca, currently living in Mexico City. My passion for cooking began at a very young age. I always remember being surrounded by good food: Oaxaca has always been a city where cooking, eating well and having fresh ingredients is very important. It's part of the culture.

When I was younger, Mexican cuisine was not as much of a world-renowned cuisine as it is now. So one of the reasons why I decided to become a chef was precisely because I saw that Mexican cuisine had extraordinary potential to grow.

When I'm cooking, what I like most is to create dishes using seasonal ingredients. I try to incorporate ancestral techniques, like using moles from my home state of Oaxaca. So my practice explores different regions of Mexico and Latin America.

For me, making Mexican food is a bit like a ritual. Many dishes, like mole and *chiles en nogada*, are ritualistic in their preparation because they involve a long list of ingredients and are complex to put together.

Arturo Sosa, Mexico City

chillies are used as a condiment in many dishes, and local fruits like tamarind, mamey and oranges are common.

Tortillas might be a regular feature in kitchens across the country, but even these vary depending on the region. In wetter central and southern Mexico, corn is plentiful, so almost all tortillas in this region are made of corn. But in northern Mexico, where the climate is much drier, wheat is the dominant crop, so Mexicans in the north tend to eat flour tortillas.

MODERN CHALLENGES

Though many of Mexico's staple ingredients and agricultural practices are still in use, they have come under threat from climate change. Soaring heat in southern Tabasco state, for example, has led to more infections among cacao plants, another core Mexican ingredient *(p104)*. The starkest estimates suggest that Mexico could lose up to 80 per cent of its fertile cropland by the end of this century. Climate change is not the only factor at play: the loss of ancestral agricultural knowledge is severely affecting the management of Mexico's farms, leading to lower crop yields and food shortages in certain regions.

The global increase in the use of industrial palm oil is also threatening Mexico's agricultural landscapes. Between 2014 and 2019, it's estimated that around 5,400 hectares (13,343 acres) of forests and jungle were lost due to the expansion of palm oil production in the areas of Chiapas, Campeche, Tabasco and Veracruz, with Mexico's mangroves *(p14)* also threatened.

Many of the country's *tortillerías*, meanwhile, have gone from producing tortillas made from nixtamalized

Above left Mexico's heirloom corn in a variety of colours

Above right *Tacos de pescado,* or fish tacos

heirloom maize to cheaper, quicker versions made with lower-quality imported corn. Mexico's corn imports tend to consist solely of industrially produced white corn, threatening the coloured varieties of heirloom crops, which can range from pale pink to golden yellow and even dark blue. Farmers have been cultivating heirloom strains for generations, and are now fortunately finding a market among consumers seeking organic produce from small-scale growers and chefs.

Mexican politicians, meanwhile, have long pushed for an outright ban on importing genetically modified corn from the US, a trade deal worth billions of dollars that has changed the way Mexicans eat.

Despite these very real threats to Mexico's food production, traditional ingredients remain at the heart of Mexican cuisine. Many of the country's best dishes are still lovingly prepared using techniques and ingredients honed thousands of years ago.

TRaDitiONaL DiSHES

From international favourites like tacos to patriotic plates such as *chiles en nogada*, Mexico makes countless incredible dishes, many of which have been cooked up for centuries. Some of these meals are everyday staples, whereas others are rolled out for special occasions – but all are absolutely delicious.

TACOS

Mexican tacos are made from a soft tortilla outer (unlike their hard-shelled American cousins) that's then packed full of flavourful fillings. There are countless ways to load a taco, perhaps with roasted pork infused with pineapple juice (*tacos al pastor*) or freshly caught fish (*tacos de pescado*). Offered by almost any street food vendor or at any market, these delightful filled pockets are a regular feature of Mexican life.

TAMALES

Long a culinary star in Mexico, these filled corn dumplings are made by adding various fillings to *masa* (corn dough) and then steaming it in corn husk leaves. The warriors and hunters of the Toltec Empire, which existed between the 10th and 12th centuries, would carry tamales with them on their journeys.

CHILAQUILES

This simple dish is a testament to the Mexican dislike of food waste. Stale tortillas are given a new lease of life by being pan fried until golden, then simmered in a chilli salsa (also often leftovers) until they go soft. Despite meaning "chilli water" in the Aztec language Nahuatl, *chilaquiles* aren't always spicy – it depends on the heat of the chilli and how much is used.

CHILES EN NOGADA

Showcasing the colours of the Mexican flag, *chiles en nogada* might be the most patriotic dish in Mexico. Fried green poblano chillies are stuffed with picadillo (a mix of chopped meat, spices and fruits), doused in a white, walnut-based cream sauce, and then sprinkled with deep-red pomegranate seeds. Created by Pueblan nuns, legend states that this dish was first served to Agustín de Iturbide, the general of the Mexican Army, after he signed the treaty asserting Mexico's independence.

MOLE

Often served alongside roasted meat and rice, this thick, rich sauce comes in near endless varieties and is commonly used as a marinade. Chillies, nuts and seeds often play a role, but beyond this recipes can differ wildly, both between and within regions. Oaxaca, for instance, is known as the land of the seven moles, with its versions including the lavish *mole negro*, containing prunes and chocolate.

1 A street food vendor in Mexico City preparing a batch of tacos

2 Corn husk leaves filled with *masa* and ready to be served

3 A plate of delicious *chilaquiles*

4 The patriotic dish of *chiles en nogada*

5 Various types of mole for sale at a market in Oaxaca City

1

2

3

4

Mole Negro

Mole Rojo

COLORA

MOLE VERDE

5

6

7

8

9

10

POZOLE

When Mexicans return to the family home for Independence Day or Christmas, a steaming saucepan of *pozole* is no doubt ready and waiting. It typically comes in three varieties (red, white and green) and is served with countless garnishes such as salsa, radishes and lime. Made from pork, hominy (or nixtamalized corn; *p81*), garlic and chillies, this soupy stew once had an unexpected ingredient: human flesh. Then, it was enjoyed by the Nahuatl-speaking rulers of the Aztec Empire at the feast of Tlacaxipehualiztli, with human prisoners sacrificed to give thanks for the harvest.

HUITLACOCHE

The blue-black fragments of what look like mushrooms in this fungal delicacy are in fact kernels of native corn. The corn is infected with *Ustilago maydis*, a pathogenic fungus that bestows a rich umami flavour. Although it's viewed as a pest in North America, corn infected by the fungus has been prized in Mexico since the Aztecs and is considered far more valuable than healthy maize. The corn is commonly served in quesadillas, soups and tacos, and can even be bought canned at Mexican grocery stores.

ESQUITES

With a name derived from the Nahuatl word *ízquitl*, meaning toasted corn, this snack has been around in some form since the days of the Aztec Empire – and its popularity shows no sign of waning. A cup of cooked corn kernels topped with mayonnaise, lime, cream, chilli powder and *cotija* cheese, it's a permanent fixture of Mexico's street food markets, and is generally eaten on the go. It is sometimes known by its alternative name, *elote en vaso*, meaning "corn in a cup".

FLAN

In Mexico's popular *comida corrida* (convenience food) restaurants, there is typically only one dessert on offer – a wonderfully wobbly, caramel-coated flan. Arriving with the Spanish in the 1500s, this ultra-sweet dessert is a Mexican favourite. Local chefs have made it their own by adding flavours such as coconut, coffee and honey to the standard egg and milk custard, which is boiled or steamed in round moulds and chilled before serving.

PESCADO ZARANDEADO

The culinary calling card of the state of Nayarit, this smoky fish dish is ideal for feeding large family groups. It has its roots in the Mesoamerican Totorame people who invented a method of grilling using wood from tropical mangroves for added flavour. Today, large white fish are still spatch-cocked and smothered in a sauce that varies from cook to cook but always involves mayonnaise and mustard, before being braised over hot coals on a wood-burning stove. The Chinese influence along the west coast of Mexico has led to soy sauce becoming a popular marinade for the cooked fish.

6 A steaming bowl of spicy red *pozole*

7 Corn infected with the fungus *Ustilago maydis*, known in the US as corn smut

8 *Esquites* served at a street market

9 Plates of flan at a food market

10 *Pescado zarandeado* (or grilled fish), topped with red onions and ready for sharing

ON THE MAP

CHILLIES

Enchilarse – to overdo it on the spice – is common in Mexico, the world's most chilli-diverse country, where *"¿Pica?"* ("Is it spicy?") is always answered with a lie: "No!" Here, chillies of all shapes and sizes show up in tacos, sweets and even shampoo, and are used to cure ear infections, ward off bad energies and aid gastritis. Here are just some of Mexico's more than 60 domesticated and hundreds of *criollo* (native) varieties.

The *chile de árbol* is a skinny, dark red and distinctly spicy variant, popularly used in Mexican chilli oils and thought to have originated in Los Altos de Jalisco (the Jaliscan Highlands), found in the state of **Jalisco**.

Chilhuacle (or *huacle*) plays a crucial role in one of Mexico's staple dishes: *mole negro* (a spicy, chocolatey black sauce). Cultivated primarily in **Oaxaca**, this rich, deep and mildly fruity chilli is now extremely expensive, and is often subbed out for the abundant *chile guajillo*.

Small but mighty, the tiny, spherical *chile chiltepín* is popularly employed by people in Mexico's **Huasteca** region, as well as by the Rarámuri, to ward off evil, and aid with muscular aches and pains, fevers, bruises and wounds. It's also commonly eaten with seafood.

Allegedly brought from Cuba by Spanish colonizers – hence the name – the habanero actually originated in South America. Now, the variant grown in the **Yucatán Peninsula** *(p11)* is Mexico's spiciest, widely used to flavour *cochinita pibil* (roasted, richly spiced pork), tongue-tingling sauces and plenty more.

Known as chipotles when dried, jalapeños are traditionally cultivated in Xalapa, **Veracruz** and – in their traditional form – are in danger of extinction. Perhaps the most well known of the Mexican chillies, jalapeños are used worldwide.

The typically mild *chile poblano*, originating in the state of **Puebla**, is the star of *chiles en nogada* (a stuffed chilli, topped with walnut sauce and pomegranate seeds) and other roasted-and-stuffed chilli dishes. When dried, it becomes *chile ancho*, used in mole.

FOOD CULTURE

How, when and where food is eaten in Mexico is just as important as the dish itself, whether it's a long and leisurely lunch around the table or a tasty taco devoured on the street.

In Mexico, food underpins all aspects of life: there's nothing that can't be solved with a quick *antojito* (snack), and bread rolls are customarily offered to calm the nerves. Long before a meal begins, a vast amount of time is spent sourcing, preparing or simply discussing food.

MARKET LIFE

Mexican food culture begins at the local municipal market or the sprawling *tianguis* (clusters of open-air, temporary vendors). Stalls here – which have their roots in the great Aztec *tianquiztli*, or ancient markets – move from neighbourhood to neighbourhood throughout the week, ensuring they serve as many locals as possible. Their arrival is often accompanied by an unmistakable cacophony: vendors calling out their wares, large speakers booming the latest chart hits and crowds of customers haggling for the best prices.

It's common to start here when food shopping, picking up staple fruits and fresh vegetables – tomatoes and avocados, both native to Mexico; chayotes, a type of squash; petite Ataulfo mangos; chillies; cactus paddles and more – before moving on to the nearby *carnicería* (butchers), *tortillería*

Aztec Food Markets

Almost every town and city throughout the Aztec Empire had a local food market. Most goods were transported by canoe, and were bought and traded using cacao beans as currency. Just some of the incredible variety of products on offer included animal hides, sharks' teeth, rubber, charcoal, olives, squashes, cactus leaves and peanuts, as well as clothing and musical instruments. The great market of Tlatelolco in the ancient city of Tenochtitlán, held daily, was estimated to attract up to 60,000 people on its busiest days.

Right A market in Tlacolula, selling a large variety of fruit and vegetables

(tortilla shop) and, eventually, the *panadería* (bakery).

That's not to say Mexicans haven't embraced big-name stores and super-markets, as well as on-demand delivery services, but the importance of main-taining a good relationship with your local vendors not only saves cash (you might even be treated to a *pilón*, or freebie, every now and again), it helps maintain community in a rapidly modernizing country (*p26*). And it's said you're not truly Mexican until you've been gifted a branded calendar by your neighbourhood tortilla, meat or fruit vendor at the end of the year. Those handouts are a badge of local honour.

FAMILY MEALS

Food may be important to Mexican culture, but family is arguably more so (*p58*). Inevitably, then, there's little Mexican families enjoy more than

bonding over cooking and eating together. Mexican families are usually delighted to invite guests for dinners, which are generally large and sumptuous affairs, and guests should *never* show up empty handed.

Family meals often begin with communal preparation, during which time-honoured family recipes are passed down to new generations. This rings especially true for complex dishes like mole (*p86*), recipes for which are often closely guarded by families. Then there are the traditional *tamaladas* (tamale parties) of the winter season, for which families will set aside whole afternoons to prepare batches of tamales (*p86*) to share out.

In the north especially, *carne asadas*, or barbecues, are often big, informal family affairs, during which some people handle the grilling, while others chop vegetables, prepare guacamole with a *molcajete* (mortar) and dish out ice-cold beers. More formal family dinners, including at Christmas, may involve elaborate set tables, smarter-than-usual dress and multiple courses.

THE SOBREMESA

Long after the meal is finished, family and friends remain at the dinner table for *platicas* (chats). The *sobremesa* (literally, "over table") may have originated in Spanish culture, but it's a concept that's been absorbed and transformed in Mexico to mean a vital time, post-dinner, to catch up, gossip, argue, smoke and maybe even enjoy a coffee, tequila and mezcal or two to round off the meal.

Importantly, there's no time limit to these leisurely *sobremesa* moments. When dining out you'll find that no one's there to hurry you along, and

there's certainly no cheque dropped on the table the minute food is finished. Even if there were, it would go ignored, with diners typically staying at their favourite restaurants long after they have been served their final course.

EATING OUT

When it comes to dining out, any time of day will do in Mexico, with hearty and filling breakfasts, long and leisurely lunches, and rich and varied dinners. Across Mexico's towns and cities, it's not uncommon to see queues of hungry early-risers waiting for their *torta de tamal* (tamale sandwich), with a mango-flavoured Boing (a popular fruit drink) or freshly prepared *jugo* (juice) in hand. When time allows, *tacos de* *canasta* (basket tacos), *chilaquiles* and eggs in a variety of combinations are breakfast staples here.

At dinner, choosing to eat out could mean a quick taco or tortas on a busy street or bustling square, or a sit-down meal at one of the country's excellent restaurants. Restaurants remain a huge part of modern Mexican food culture, with tables spilling out onto the pavements across the country at all times of the day.

For many Mexicans, however, changing work schedules have meant eating out is now a necessity rather than a choice. The difference in dining customs between bigger, urban centres and smaller rural areas is a marker of rapid modernization. For commuters in

BEST STREET FOOD DISHES

Tortas ahogadas
A messy, spicy Guadalajara speciality, "drowned sandwiches" combine crusty *birote* bread with sizzling pork *carnitas* (crispy, lard-fried pork), pickled red onion and a red-hot sauce.

Tlacoyos
One of Mexico's myriad maize-based snacks, these oval-shaped discs of dough are stuffed with *habas* (fava beans), *requesón* (soft cheese) or *chicharrón* (pork rind), and topped with salsa, *nopales* (cactus paddles) and cheese.

Elotes
Corn-on-the-cob slathered in sour cream or mayo, plus chilli powder, cheese and a good squeeze of lime.

Raspados
Stacks of shaved ice drizzled in sugary-sweet fruit syrups and, depending on where you are, condensed milk, *raspados* are perfect for the heat.

Dogos
Sonoran staples, *dogos* (hotdogs) are wrapped in bacon, served in a bun, and topped with beans, tomato, onion, mustard and – most importantly – crumbled potato chips, among other things.

bigger cities, long travel times and longer work days mean sitting down for a meal isn't an option, with at-home egg dishes subbed out for on-the-go sandwiches and street food snacks, *licuados* (smoothies) and instant coffee.

Local workers will also make use of *comida corrida*, literally "fast food", served at their local cafeteria, street food stand or *fonda*. Small, often family-run *fonda* are found across the country, from the old heart of Mexico City to the rural villages of the Yucatán Peninsula. These counters – originally staples of working-class culture before their appeal spread to more affluent urban neighbourhoods – provide a vital social outlet in what could otherwise seem an anonymous urban environment. It's not unusual for busy workers to enjoy three quick courses dished out in rapid-fire fashion at a nearby *fonda*.

STREET FOOD
While lunch counters typically close by mid-afternoon, Mexico's plethora of street food joints remain open well into the night. These outdoor food vendors are a product of the country's late 19th-century industrialization, when hungry factory workers would be served cheap cuts of meat and basic vegetables from an array of pop-up stalls. The street food itself, as diverse as its people, remains the lifeblood of the country's food culture.

Now often dubbed "*Vitamina T*" for the abundance of "t" snacks (think tacos, tortas, *tostadas*, *tlacoyos*,

Above left Sweet fried churros coated in sugar at a *churrería*

Above right A taco served at a local food market

tamales), savoury street food generally combines corn, meat, cheese and chillies in varying configurations. It fuels the nation, and snacking on affordable, delicious and often more-nutritious-than-you-might-think dishes is enjoyed by practically everyone, regardless of class or income.

It's estimated that around 75 per cent of Mexico's urban population eat street food at least once a week, with food served off the back of bicycles, out of shop windows or from graffiti-strewn food trucks blaring hip-hop. You can barely turn a corner in towns and cities across Mexico without stumbling upon a señora perched on a plastic stool beside a *comal* (griddle), hand-shaping gorditas (stuffed dough discs) or shredding cheese for quesadillas; ditto a churros seller frying tubes of sweet, sugar-coated dough in deep vats of oil. There is no better place to experience the unique wonders of Mexican cuisine than on the street. After all, it's where the entire country comes to eat.

TIME

for

TACOS

Eaten morning, noon and night countrywide, tacos are allegedly enjoyed by half of all Mexicans at least once a week. On average, everybody in Mexico is believed to live roughly 400 m (1,300 ft) from one of the country's some 50,000 taco stands. In short, they're a (ubiquitous) national treasure.

From limited-time-only taco stands assembled in the morning and packed up by afternoon, to 24/7 aluminium *puestos* with rotating spits of marinated pork, taco vendors run the gamut. The meats, fillings and salsa-spiciness may differ from region to region, but some things are inevitable: expect diners perched on flimsy plastic stools, demonstrating the taco-eating head tilt that keeps the filling contained; metal bowls overflowing with spicy salsas and hunks of lime; and steaming griddles full of freshly grilled meats and soft tortillas. That's not forgetting the (typically male) *taquero*'s siren call of *"¿Qué le damos?"* ("What'll it be?"), followed by *"¿Con todo?"* ("With onion and coriander?").

While Mexican street food culture dates back to around 15th-century Tenochtitlán, the history of tacos is murky. Some pin them to the 18th-century silver mines, others to Aztec emperor Moctezuma's use of tortillas as a spoon. Whatever the case, these days, vendors reign over their individual street corners, or cluster near the competition to provide a smorgasbord of taco-tasting options. Decorated with their traditional *rótulos* (colourful, hand-painted signs), the country's taco stands are a permanent fixture.

A GLOBAL MENU

Given the country's fresh ingredients and bold flavours, it's little surprise that Mexico has shaped the world's cuisine, with a recipe book inspired by centuries of global exchange.

Mexican food is one of the country's greatest exports, and its fiery flavours have found a home around the world. Yet this influence has never been a one-way street: Mexico's cuisine has likewise been shaped by the arrival of peoples who carried the flavours and ingredients of home.

TEX-MEX AND BORDER FOOD

Many people from outside of Mexico first encounter the country's food through the broad cross-border fusion known as Tex-Mex. This cuisine was created by Tejanos – Texans of Spanish or Mexican heritage – who took Mexican dishes and gave them a southwestern twist in the late 1800s. Steaming vats of chilli con carne became a popular sight in San Antonio in the 1880s – the dish was hearty, cheap and warming. Tejanos added ingredients less commonly found in Mexican cooking, but which were abundant in Texas, including beef, black beans, cheese and cumin. This gave rise to classics such as burritos, breakfast tacos and cheese enchiladas, which are now common features in restaurants throughout the US and beyond.

While it's true that some dishes have become commercialized, with countless American chain restaurants serving hard taco shells that little resemble their Mexican cousins, Tex-Mex is very much a cuisine in its own right. It beautifully blends ingredients and cooking styles together, one reason why it's the most popular cuisine in the US. Today, even

Left Tacos and nachos served at a Mexican restaurant

Right A Mexican restaurant in California, a popular sight across the US

HEROES OF TEX-MEX

Burritos

Much like their Mexican cousins, Tex-Mex burritos are made from a tortilla packed with fillings. But, unlike Mexican burritos, which are filled with the likes of refried beans and a sprinkling of cheese, Tex-Mex offerings are packed with items like rice and veggies, topped with sour cream, and generally much larger in size.

Breakfast tacos

A staple of Tex-Mex cuisine, breakfast tacos are typically made up of scrambled eggs with cheese, meat or other accoutrements in a soft, warm tortilla. While similar egg-based variations exist in Mexico's northern states, you won't find anything quite like it in the rest of the country.

Enchiladas

Think of this as the baked version of Mexican enchiladas. While the originals are dipped in chilli sauce, filled with white cheese and then topped with sour cream, lettuce and tomato, the Tex-Mex version is filled with cheese, chicken and beef, and generously smothered in a chilli-tomato sauce before baking.

non-Tejano dishes are considered Tex-Mex, such as the chimichanga (essentially a version of a quesadilla) which was invented in an Arizona restaurant. Other distinctions between Mexican and Tex-Mex recipes include the use of black beans over pinto beans in the US, and the reliance on cumin north of the border (the spice is rarely used in Mexican cooking).

Cross-border fusion between the US and Mexico doesn't end with Tex-Mex, however. Thanks to a large Mexican population, California is home to an array of Mexican-influenced dishes. Some are hearty, such as *carne asada* fries (crispy french fries topped with things like cheddar cheese, *carne asada* and *pico de gallo*); others offer a much lighter take on Mexican favourites, with so-called "Cal-Mex" focused on seafood or plant-based recipes.

GLOBAL INFLUENCE

Mexico's reach stretches much further than the US, however, especially when it comes to the classic ingredients it has made globally popular. Key components of Mexican cuisine made their way to Europe on Spanish ships, meaning the country's most important ingredients – including corn, beans and chilli – are now found the world over. The same holds true for ingredients like cacao (*p104*), vanilla, pineapples and avocado – even if they do need to be imported from Mexico and other countries across Central and South America.

Some Mexican ingredients have become so well assimilated into other country's cuisines that we don't think of them as being Mexican: tomatoes form an important part of Italian cooking and yet were only introduced into the country, by way of Spain, in 1548.

The same could be said for the use of chillies. Historians estimate that the first chilli pepper was domesticated in central east Mexico around 6,000 years ago, and the spicy peppers were subsequently brought over to Europe in the late 15th century. Originally used as an exotic-looking plant to decorate gardens, the Portuguese realized that the pepper could be used to add spice to cuisine, and European diets were changed irrevocably as a result. The spread of the chilli pepper would change diets around the world; we might now associate Chinese cooking with the chilli, but chilli peppers didn't reach the country until the 16th century.

A CHANGING DIET

The tides of history have also influenced Mexico's cuisine within the country's

borders. As part of the transatlantic slave trade, the Spanish brought an estimated 200,000 enslaved people from Africa to work on plantations during the colonial era. These enslaved people brought with them both ingredients and ways of cooking that continue to influence Mexican cuisine. Sesame seeds, sometimes sprinkled over mole, were introduced by this group, as were hibiscus flowers, used today to make *agua de jamaica*. Plantains are especially popular, being used in dishes such as breakfast favourite *huevos motuleños* and the sweet *plátanos fritos*; they are especially popular in places that have large Afro-Mexican populations, such as Veracruz, where they're used to make dough for gorditas and empanadas.

Other immigrant groups have made a substantial impact on Mexican cuisine, too. In the late 19th century, for instance, many Chinese labourers were enticed by lucrative payment for working on Mexico's new railways. Their arrival saw a number of fusion dishes born, especially in the border state of Baja California. Items on the menu here include *carnitas coloradas* (barbecue pork) and Chinese fried rice served with avocado. Many more international influences are apparent across the country, whether it's Mexico City's Lebanese-influenced *tacos al pastor*, Puebla's *tacos árabes* (developed out of Iraqi kebabs) or Guadalajara's famed *birote* – a sourdough twist on the French baguette.

CACAO

Chocolate is now celebrated around the world, but it was the Olmecs who first domesticated its source, cacao. Though cacao isn't native to Mexico, hailing instead from the Amazon, the first evidence we have of people roasting, fermenting and grinding the seeds of the fruit is traces found on Olmec pots in modern-day Tabasco and Veracruz, dating from 1500 BCE.

Whether cacao was originally domesticated for consumption or for spiritual offerings is a matter of debate. It was the Mayans who began incorporating "the food of the gods" into religious rituals around 250 CE, burying corpses with it and even using it instead of rings to seal marriage ceremonies. The Aztec rulers, meanwhile, accepted cacao beans in the 15th century as tribute payments from the heads of smaller states throughout the empire.

Historians tend to disagree over exactly when cacao travelled from the Americas to Europe, though there is general agreement that it first arrived in Spain. Some stories trace its arrival back to Christopher Columbus, while others claim cacao was brought back from Mexico by Spanish conquistador Hernán Cortés. Whoever it arrived with, it didn't take long for chocolate to become a highly sought-after delicacy in Spain, and word quickly spread to other European countries. By the 17th century, the entire world had discovered the joys of chocolate.

Above Fields of agave, the main ingredient in tequila

Left Tequila bottles displayed at a rural cantina

Mexican Spirits

Mexican food might be known the world over, but every dish is made better when it's accompanied by a great drink, and the country's bars and cantinas are stocked with a wide assortment of wonders.

Mexico is a treasure trove of innovative alcoholic drinks, each a synthesis of time-honoured wisdom and modern experimentation. Tequila and its smokier cousin, mezcal, are truly world renowned, with stringent rules governing their production every bit as strict as those governing French cognac or US bourbon.

MIGHTY MEZCAL

Many of Mexico's most celebrated spirits owe their existence to a single species of plant: agave. The fermented sap of the plant has been consumed in Mexico since at least the era of the Aztecs, who revered maguey (a species of the agave family) as a symbol of abundance. Maguey was closely associated with the Aztec deity Mayahuel, goddess of fertility, and the consumption of spirits made from maguey's fermented sap – most notably pulque, a white and frothy beverage with a distinctly sour taste – was linked with a variety of spiritual rituals.

Mezcal is the general name for any spirit made from agave, which grows throughout Mexico and the south-western US. Tequila is in fact a member

of the mezcal family, but tequila can only be made from the blue agave. A mezcal, on the other hand, is made from any other agave plant, of which there are about 200 (though only around 30 are suitable for making a palatable mezcal).

Mezcal in Crisis

The recent mezcal boom has exposed a number of problems with agave-based spirit production. On average agave takes 15 years to reach maturity, so it's hard for producers to meet rising demand. The process of roasting mezcal agaves in pits also uses far more wood than the roasting of blue agaves for tequila in brick ovens, which is contributing to severe deforestation in large parts of rural Mexico. In something of a vicious cycle, this is exacerbated by the tearing out of yet more forests for space to plant additional agaves.

Mezcal's characteristic smokiness arises when the agave plants are cooked in deep pits lined with heated rocks, a complex distillation process that long predated the arrival of Spanish conquistadors. The pits are then filled with wood and charcoal to ensure even cooking. Indeed, the very word "mezcal" derives from the word *mexcalli* from the Indigenous Nahua people, meaning "oven-cooked agave".

There are regional variations of mezcal, made from an array of local agave plants. Bacanora, for example, made in the state of Sonora, was known for many years as "Mexican moonshine". In the early 19th century, the governor of Sonora outlawed its production, fearing its consumption was contribu-ting to a rising wave of local hedonism, and the spirit remained prohibited until the Mexican govern-ment overturned the ban in 1992.

HISTORY OF TEQUILA

Tequila was for a period just another type of mezcal, but in the 19th century discerning drinkers became aware of a distinction: the spirit produced around the town of Tequila, in the state of Jalisco, tasted smoother than those produced elsewhere, largely due to the area's effective distillation of blue agave. This premium variety was named after the town, though the tequila of today comes from a far wider area, specifically the states of Guanajuato, Michoacán, Nayarit, Tamaulipas and Jalisco.

As the drink became more popular, more *tabernas* (distilleries) sprang up in the late 19th century, often named after their owners or, later, after virtuous characteristics such as perseverance or loyalty. Tequila was first exported to the US in 1873, and sales quickly grew with the expansion of the railways. This popularity led to the development of the tequila-based margarita cocktail, though the drink has more apocryphal origin stories and claimed "inventors" than perhaps any other *(p112)*.

The production of tequila is now strictly regulated by the Mexican government. In fact, the very term "tequila" is deemed to be the govern-ment's intellectual property. It must be made from at least 51 per cent blue agave; tequilas that are 100 per cent blue agave are deemed to be of the highest quality.

A LOADED BAR

Tequila and mezcal might hog the limelight, but Mexico has many other spirits worth sampling *(p110)*. One such spirit is rum: Mexico produces more rum than all Caribbean countries combined, many with unique flavour profiles and methods of distillation. Sugar cane, a central ingredient of rum, grows throughout Mexico's Gulf and Pacific coasts and makes up the country's second-largest crop area after corn. Throughout the 21st century, Mexico

Above A distiller standing next to his equipment

has also seen a boom in popularity of one of the world's most ubiquitous spirits, whisky (spelled without the "e"). In true Mexican style, the country's whisky is almost all made with corn, and is an increasingly popular way of using up any surplus of the country's most ubiquitous crop. This popularity has spread beyond Mexico's border, with sales of Mexican whisky booming in the US.

Of course, it's not just spirits that you'll find in the country's best bars. First introduced to the country in the 19th century by German and Austrian immigrants, beer is by far the most popular alcoholic beverage in Mexico today. While some of it is mass-produced by internationally owned companies (think Corona), there's also been a rise in the number of craft breweries. In fact, many big cities are home to myriad boundary-pushing brewers, especially on the Baja Peninsula, many of whom focus on creating new offerings using the finest local ingredients.

ON THE MAP

DIFFERENT SPIRITS

Every region of Mexico has its own beloved spirit, the product of the best local crops and fruits. Recipes are closely guarded, with lively origin stories traded over glasses in local cantinas. By merging centuries of ancestral wisdom with cutting-edge techniques, distillers are finding new fans around the world. Here are some of the highlights from Mexico's extensive drinks menu.

Sotol is made from the desert spoon plant, which in Mexico grows mainly in the Chihuahuan Desert, found in **Chihuahua** state. As the agave shortage continues to cause concern for tequila and mezcal distillers, many are looking to *sotol* as the future hero of Mexican spirits. _____

Pox, pronounced "poshe", was originally a ceremonial drink of the Tsotzil people who lived in the highlands of **Chiapas** (the term means "healing" in the Tsotzil language). It's traditionally made from corn and cacao beans, though there is no single way to produce it.

The Mexican version of eggnog, *rompope* is based on a combination of rum or brandy, milk, sugar and egg yolks, and is now popular across Latin America. It's believed that the first version of *rompope* was created in **Puebla** by the Santa Clara nuns, however, sometime in the 1600s.

Hailing from the **Yucatán Peninsula (p11)**, *Kalani* is a liqueur made with Mexican sugar-cane rum and fresh coconut milk, extracted from local coconuts. A newer addition to Mexico's spirit scene, artisanal distillers are experimenting with *Kalani* cocktails, giving a Mexican twist to favourites like the Mai Tai.

Charanda, a rum-like spirit, hails from the state of **Michoacán**, where it's made from the abundant sugarcane growing in the state's central valley. The area has uniquely iron-rich soil, giving *charanda* green tropical notes and a lingering freshness.

Like mezcal, *comiteco* is distilled from agave sap, though unlike its relative the agave is fermented but never roasted. Exclusively made in the state of **Chiapas**, the spirit was outlawed in the 1960s due to a shortage of agave plants. Since the ban was lifted in the 1990s, it has become a popular artisanal spirit.

MYTHS
of the
MARGARITA

It might be one of the world's most popular cocktails, but no one can say for certain who invented the margarita, a drink whose key ingredient is tequila. Tales have circulated for over a century, with various places and people proudly declaring the cocktail their own invention. Was it a gift from a doting lover to Marguerite, his tequila-loving sweetheart? Or was it perhaps the 19th-century concoction of the world's foremost tequila brand, Jose Cuervo, which was largely responsible for bringing tequila from Mexico to the US? Another origin story links the sour drink to the Daisy cocktail popular in the US in the early 20th century ("*margarita*" means "daisy" in Spanish).

The first concrete evidence we have of a margarita-like cocktail appeared not in Mexico but in Britain in 1937. British author William Tarling's *Café Royal Cocktail Book* featured a recipe for a Picador which used identical ingredients to the margarita as we know it today: tequila, orange liqueur and lime juice. And in Mexico? The iconic Tommy's Place Bar, in Juárez, is celebrated as the first place to serve the drink under its now familiar name in 1942. The region now claims to make the best margaritas in the world.

As it spread across the world in the latter half of the 20th century, the recipe has barely changed, testament to the enduring popularity of Mexico's favourite spirit. Its origins might be hazy, but one thing's for sure: the margarita could never have existed without tequila.

DRiNK CULtURe

Birthdays, holidays, Fridays: with Mexico's ready availability of tipples, there's a drink to mark any occasion, and often a dedicated place in which to enjoy it.

Drinks have been a key part of the Mexican social fabric since the days of the Mesoamerican empires. Whether used in rituals or simply to toast the weekend, the country's drinks offer far more than refreshment.

PULQUERÍA PASSION

Few drinks capture the development of Mexico's drinking culture quite like pulque (p107). For the Aztecs, the sacred drink was used in ceremonies by priests, who were the only individuals permitted to enjoy it. After the arrival of the Spanish, however, pulque became more commonly consumed (albeit mostly by men), as the conquistadors pushed to secularize the drink. Bars dedicated to pulque, known as *pulquerías*, were established. These bars tended to be men-only, partly because the drink was associated with virility; sometimes colloquially known as "Mexican viagra", it's still considered a natural aphrodisiac by some.

Pulquerías were particularly popular in the late 19th and early 20th centuries, with members of the working class visiting after work to enjoy pulque poured from traditional *cacarizas* (pitchers). Over the course of the 20th century, pulque's popularity declined, in part due to competition from Mexico's large beer manufacturers. Today, however, the drink is seeing a revival, especially among younger people, as a more locally made alternative to beer (it has a similar alcohol content) and as a cheaper option than mezcal. It's led to the country's *pulquerías* becoming popular once again, with these once men-only bars now welcoming everyone.

CANTINA SOCIETY

Mexico's cantinas have seen a similar resurgence. Emerging during the mid-19th century, these bars were social spaces exclusively for men, and were seen as hotbeds of machismo: drinkers could compete at dominoes, discuss the day's labour, eat on-the-house *botanas* (bar snacks) and, of course, sink a few beers or tequilas.

The heyday of the traditional cantina came in the 1940s and 1950s. Mexican cinema romanticized their smoke-filled interiors, with war heroes trading tales of the revolution and poets penning verse

Above Cantinas on Calle 59, in the old town of Campeche

Right Pulque enjoyed at a *pulquería*

---

on beer barrels. They began to lose favour in subsequent decades, due in part to newer European-inspired bars and bistros taking their place. Hundreds of old and crumbling cantinas dotted the centre of Mexico's cities, a once-bustling cornerstone of society that became a relic of a bygone age.

In the late 20th century, however, the faded glamour of the cantina was ripe for reclaiming, and the bars became hip favourites, with many being lovingly restored. Women were given permission to enter in 1981 as part of a broader push for gender equality. Today, everyone from friends to families spills through their doors, and drinks can be accompanied by live mariachi music or coin-operated jukeboxes. Many traditional cantinas have become proudly modern spaces, with weekend DJs and gourmet small plates served alongside artisanal tequilas and local lagers. However, there are still some rural areas where macho attitudes persist and cantinas are regarded as strictly men-only, if just by custom alone.

RAISING A GLASS

Though Mexico has a fondness for its watering holes, alcohol isn't confined to the cantina. In fact, alcoholic drinks are a centrepiece of numerous social occasions. At Mexican weddings, for instance, open bars are regarded as a given and alcohol-fuelled after-parties a must. Christmas is another reason to raise a glass, with many Mexicans nursing traditional drinks such as *rompope (p111)*. In fact, the Mexican holiday season is an excuse to dust off a host of festive spirits, including *Ponche Navideño*, a spiced fruit punch that can be alcohol-free or taken *con piquete* (topped up with tequila or brandy).

It's not just special occasions that warrant a tipple and a cry of "*¡Salud!*".

Cheers!

Mexicans love a good toast, or *brindis*, when drinking. There's the entry-level toast – "*¡Salud!*" – and then there are the specifics, including: "*¡Que vivan los novios!*" ("Long live the bride and groom"), used to toast the happy couple at weddings. And for spirits, "*Pa' arriba, pa' abajo, pal centro, pa' dentro!*" ("Up, down, into the middle and down the hatch!"), plus accompanying hand movements, is a common cantina refrain. And a key rule? Always look the person saying "cheers" in the eye.

Everyday socializing is deeply intertwined with alcohol in Mexico. Whether grabbing after-work beers with colleagues or sampling tequila with friends at *antros* (clubs), especially in urban areas, drinking alcohol is a social rite of passage throughout the country. Often, for the younger generation, nights of drinking end in a dance circle or by taking part in a *pulpo* (literally, "octopus"), essentially the act of interlinking arms with someone before downing your respective drinks.

SOMETHING LIGHTER

It isn't only alcohol that's integral to Mexican society, of course. In summer, perhaps the most frequented drinking spot will be the *agua frescas* vendor at the local market, visited throughout the day by shoppers as they run errands. The drink is served by the litre or half-litre from large honeypot-shaped plastic vats, with many Mexicans on friendly terms with their local stallholder.

And then there's the local café, a social hub across every Mexican state. Unlike in many other countries, coffee in Mexico is seen as both a daytime and an evening drink, with cafés open late and milkier varieties like the cappuccino enjoyed well into the evening. Though many Mexicans brew coffee at home, ordering one at a café serves a more fundamental purpose: it facilitates communication and brings the local community together, drink in hand. In Mexico, there's no better way to bond.

DRiNKS LiSt

Mexico's spirits may be world famous but its soft drinks are equally exciting and innovative – and all too often overlooked. Using complex processes refined over generations, the best local produce is fermented, stirred and mixed to form uniquely delicious drinks.

TEJATE

Tejate is a special blend of toasted corn, fermented cacao beans, pixtle (toasted seeds from the mamey fruit) and cacao flowers, all ground into a chocolate-coloured paste and mixed with water. Known as "the drink of the gods", *Tejate* has been made in the Oaxaca region by the Zapotec peoples for centuries. Walk through the markets of Oaxaca today and it's impossible to miss the vendors pouring streams of frothy liquid from painted gourds into cups. The cacao flowers rise to the surface, forming the drink's signature foam top.

POZOL

Known as "the drink you can eat" in Tabasco, where it originates, this Meso-american mixture of *masa* (nixtamalized maize dough) and ground cacao has always been popular with farmers and merchants. After the sour liquid is drunk, a gritty residue known as "shish" is left, which makes for a tasty snack. As well as the cacao version, it's common to mix it with sweet potato or to ferment the *masa* for up to five days for added tang. The drink has long been used for sustenance on long journeys by Indigenous peoples.

CAFÉ DE OLLA

Although coffee was only introduced to Mexico in the 18th century, it has quickly become a staple and most rural families have their own *café de olla* (meaning "pot coffee") recipe. Legend has it that this drink was born during the Mexican Revolution when thrifty women reheated leftover coffee in a clay pot with spices such as cinnamon and cloves as well as plenty of brown sugar to keep men on the front line alert through the night. Although it can be made in a saucepan, locals prefer traditional clay pots which add a mineral, earthy flavour. Traditional *café de olla* is now less common than regular coffee in Mexico's cities.

ATOLE

This comforting, custard-like drink is often consumed for breakfast or before bed, particularly in the colder winter months. Invented by the Aztecs and traditionally served on feast days such as Día de los Muertos *(p190)* and Día de la Candelaria *(p200)*, it's made from corn-starch diluted with milk. Many regions have their own varieties: blackberries are added in Michoacán, sunflower seeds in Queretaro; in Guerrero it's served cold and combined with cinnamon, rice and cacao. A chocolate version of *atole* is more commonly known as a *champurrado*.

1 A vat of chocolate-coloured *tejate* in Mexico City

2 *Pozol* being served at a market

3 A clay mug of coffee: many Mexicans prefer the flavour imparted by clay pots and mugs

4 *Atole* chefs, known as *pascuales*, preparing a large vat of *atole* during the *danza de los arrieros*, a traditional fiesta dance

XOCOLATL

Historians believe the Mayans used cacao as both a health tonic and as a drink in a variety of rituals. When the Aztecs conquered the Mayans they forced them to pay taxes in cacao beans, and began to brew the ancient hot chocolate known as *xocolatl* with spices like cinnamon and chilli for added kick. These remain the primary flavour profiles, and the drink is poured from cup to cup before serving to aerate the cacao and create a velvety texture. The English name "chocolate" is derived from the Nahuatl word *xocolatl*, meaning "bitter water".

AGUA FRESCAS

Translating as "fresh waters", these refreshing favourites combine water with tropical ingredients and are generally served in two sizes: *chico* (0.5 l) or *grande* (1 l). Popular choices include tamarind, hibiscus flower, lemon with chia seeds and *horchata* (rice and cinnamon with a milky consistency). All are served with ice and sugar, perfect for fighting off the fierce Mexican heat.

TEJUINO

With a flavour profile similar to a Bloody Mary, this saline, sour drink, made from fermented corn and lime juice, is a street food favourite. In Jalisco, it's topped with zingy lime sorbet and chilli flakes, while in Colima in western Mexico, it's poured over crushed ice, drizzled with extra lime and dusted with salt.

TEPACHE

The slightly fizzy, probiotic-rich drink called *tepache* has existed among Mexico's Indigenous peoples for hundreds of years. Although *tepache* comes from a Nahuatl word which translates as "drink made from corn", it's thought the Mayans also had an equivalent that they brewed with sacred herbs during ceremonies. Today's *tepache* is made from fermenting the pulp and skin of pineapples for up to three days. It's often served at food and drink markets with floating chunks of fresh fruit, providing sweetness in an otherwise fairly sour experience.

5 A steaming cup of *xocolatl*

6 Large vats of *agua frescas* in a variety of flavours, for sale at a food market

7 A market seller offering fresh *tejuino*

8 *Tepache* served in cups and bags

ENTERTAINING MEXICO

Clocking up some of the highest working hours in the world, Mexicans need their downtime. Thankfully, there's plenty of entertainment on offer: the jaunty rhythms of mariachi bands, the high-action antics of lucha libre matches and the melodramatic storylines of the country's beloved telenovelas. But kicking back in Mexico sometimes goes beyond pure amusement, with entertainment offering a lens through which to discuss challenging issues; here, award-winning films cover corruption, poverty and violence, while comedians ruthlessly mock politicians. Such an enduring ability to both entertain and inform has given the likes of Mexican cinema, music and television a global appeal, and what's entertaining Mexico is now entertaining the world.

MUSiC

When it comes to keeping Mexico entertained, music leads the way. There's mariachi, of course, but beyond this iconic genre is a diverse repertoire of styles, from lyrical corridos to fast-paced rap.

Whether it's the joyful tunes of mariachi or edgy, punk-inspired rock beats, the country's musicians love to entertain. Mexico is home to an array of genres, many of which blend Indigenous, Spanish and African influences.

MESOAMERICAN MUSIC

Music was important to Mesoamerican groups such as the Aztecs, who used it in religious and spiritual ceremonies or war chants. These groups made instruments out of wood, clay and animal-based items, and often re-created natural sounds – such as thunder – in their music.

During the 16th century, new sounds were born, most specifically *el son*. This broad style of music blended the Baroque music of Spain with Indigenous and African sounds, the latter provided by enslaved peoples who arrived in Mexico with the Spanish. Played as a form of entertainment or during social gatherings, *el son* developed over the following centuries as a form of fast-paced folk music, with lyrics focusing on topics such as love, legends, well-known figures and political events. Performers also sang about land and animals, which were important aspects of most Mexicans' pastoral way of life; this focus ties back to Mesoamerican groups, who used music in agricultural fertility ceremonies.

Above A mariachi violinist performs

Above left A mariachi band playing for a wedding celebration

Different regions developed their own versions of *el son*: there's *son huasteco*, which hails from the Huasteca region and features a high falsetto singing voice and improvised violin ornamentations, and the Gulf Coast's *son jarocho*, a style known for its syncopation and repetition. On the Pacific coast was *son jalisciense*, which incorporated Spanish instruments such as guitars. Eventually, this inspired Mexico's most famous style: mariachi.

MARIACHI TO THE FORE

In the 19th century, many *son jalisciense* bands began to use a *guitarrón* (a big fretless six-string bass guitar), a *vihuela* (a high-pitched, five-stringed guitar) and two violins – three key instruments in mariachi. But the style we know today emerged in the 20th century, when now-iconic trumpets were added to the mix.

Above Rubén Albarrán, lead singer of Cafe Tacvba

Above right Mexican *rapero* (rapper) Aczino

While mariachi slowly grew in popularity, it was only following the Mexican Revolution that the style really rose to prominence. Seeking a way to encourage unity and a national identity, the Mexican government began to promote the style as an emblem of Mexico, using *mariacheros* (mariachi musicians) at political events and even subsidizing the genre. During this time, bands began to dress in a set uniform, that of a Mexican charro (cowboy), an outfit seen to convey national pride.

The style's popularization on film, television and radio from the 1920s onwards also helped to spread the genre throughout Mexico, into the US and beyond. Many mariachi bands were influenced by international styles and began incorporating other musical elements, like that of American jazz and Cuban music. Nowadays, mariachi bands are a regular feature at big events – weddings, birthdays and the like – and remain an enduring symbol of the country.

THE CORRIDO

Mariachi may be most often associated with Mexico, but it's corridos that recount the country's story. Also falling under the *son* category, this ballad-esque style emerged in the 18th century, created by travelling musicians who composed songs about important people and events – both as a form of entertainment and as a means to spread information. The narrative songs increased in popularity during the Mexican Revolution, when they were used as a way to carry news about battle outcomes and war heroes.

Yet corridos such as "La toma de Zacatecas" not only recounted the conflict; they also stoked a patriotic fire in the hearts of many Mexicans, by using descriptive lyrics to showcase examples of national pride and strength. Themes of *machismo* (including risky behaviour, drinking and womanizing) also featured during the early 20th century. Yet women

The US's influence on Mexican music continued during the rest of the 20th century. In the late 1980s, for instance, American hip-hop and street rap sparked the start of Mexican rap. Now a thriving genre, Mexican *raperos* (rappers) merge rhymes over heavy hip-hop beats, sometimes adding in traditional instrumentation, like brassy tubas and folk guitar melodies.

Today, Mexican musicians continue to draw on both international influences and the rich musical heritage of their country, creating new styles like *corridos tumbados (p130)* that are – as with mariachi before them – gaining attention around the world. This creative energy, coupled with the fact that Mexico has become the world's biggest Spanish-language music market, means that Mexican music looks set to shine even brighter in the spotlight in future.

have a significant role in the canon, too, with songs such as "La Cucaracha" and "La Adelita" recounting the indispensible participation of women in the revolution.

MODERN MEXICAN MUSIC

Although regional music remains popular, modern Mexican music has also drawn inspiration from global styles to create new and engaging sounds. Many musical influences have arrived from across the border in the US. In the late 1950s, for instance, the band Los Locos del Ritmo helped popularize rock and roll in Mexico, with guitar-led tunes and Spanish lyrics. This influenced later Mexican artists, who put their own spin on rock music, with bands such as Caifanes blending Latin percussion with new-wave styles, while the likes of Cafe Tacvba merged rock beats with punk, electronic and Indigenous folk music.

Narcocorridos

Corridos often pay homage to powerful individuals, something that has led to the rise of *narcocorridos*. These songs broadcast tales of drug lords and their exploits, focusing on things like legendary cartel operations or bloody shootouts. As stories of money, drugs and murder are regular themes in this controversial subgenre, some Mexican states – including Sinaloa, home of cartel boss El Chapo – have taken action to ban their dissemination, due to concerns they help justify crime.

ON THE MAP

MUSIC STYLES

A medley of musical styles are found peppered across the country. Some have their roots in Indigenous and Spanish heritage, while others are inspired by the sounds of the US, Cuba and beyond. This map gives a flavour of Mexico's vast musical diversity.

Dominating Mexican billboards in the early 2000s, *duranguense* is noted for its quick-paced style and use of the electronic keyboard. Interestingly, the style was first created in Chicago, Illinois by immigrants from Mexico's **Durango** state; it's since made its way back to Mexico, where it's become hugely popular.

The P'urhépecha, an Indigenous group who live in **Michoacán**, are known for *pirekuas*, songs that have been passed down orally over generations. With gentle rhythms, these songs can be sung solo, in duets or trios, or as a group. The symbolic lyrics centre on a variety of subjects, including history, human nature, politics and love.

Born along **Veracruz's** Gulf Coast, *son jarocho* was made by West African people as a form of musical resistance to their Spanish oppressors. Its speedy guitar rhythms and playful lyrics are often accompanied by *zapateado* (percussive foot-tapping and stomping), which is performed on wooden platforms to enhance the rapid drum-like sounds.

Inspired by a medley of genres, including Cuban clave and bolero, *Yucatecan trova* is one of the best-known music styles on the **Yucatán Peninsula** *(p11)*. Played using a guitar, bass and *requinto* (a small guitar with a higher-pitched sound), most songs revolve around romance. In fact, men often hire *trova* trios to serenade their significant others.

Hailing from **Oaxaca's** Isthmus of Tehuantepec, the melancholic sounds of *son istmeño* explore themes of love, heartbreak and death. The traditional arrangement includes three types of guitars – each tuned to a different key – and three vocalists, who often sing in the Zapotec language.

129

CORRIDOS TUMBADOS

In 2019, a new style of Mexican music emerged: *corridos tumbados*. Young musicians such as Natanael Cano began to mix traditional corridos – narrative songs that recount epic stories – with trap music, a subgenre of hip-hop from the US. While "tumbado" loosely translates as "knocked or pushed over", this fresh style honours its musical roots, keeping the detailed storytelling and folksy instrumentation of the traditional corrido, but enhancing it with trap beats and edgy lyrics.

Much like *narcocorridos (p127)*, *corridos tumbados* – also known as *trap corrido* – is regarded as a somewhat controversial genre, due to gritty lyrics that glamorize things like drug taking, violence and crime. Yet many artists who have taken up this new style sing about other issues too, including love, heartbreak and a longing for a life of ease and luxury. These are topics that strike a chord with the younger generation – most listeners are under 25 years old – perhaps due to the sense of disenchantment, rebellion and desire for change that they can often convey.

Although *corridos tumbados* are distinctly Mexican, they have caught the ear of music lovers around the world, especially in the US, Guatemala, Colombia and Spain. Some songs have broken international streaming records, such as "Ella baila sola" ("She Dances Alone"), a song from the Guadalajara-born artist Peso Pluma *(pictured)*. And with top *corridos tumbados* artists now bringing new genres, such as reggaeton and mariachi, into the mix, the stage is set for this new style – and Mexican music in general – to keep evolving.

ON THE BIG SCREEN

For over a century, Mexican film-makers have been delighting moviegoers at home and abroad, creating iconic moments in cinema history and gifting the industry with some of its most celebrated artists.

Dating to the early 20th century, the country's rich history of film-making has long received international acclaim. From its heyday in the 1940s and 1950s through to the contemporary wave of Mexican directors and actors who have triumphed in Hollywood, cinema is one of Mexico's greatest cultural exports.

THE GOLDEN AGE

Although cinema emerged in the country in the late 19th century, film-making truly began to flourish in the 1930s, instigating what is known as the Golden Age of Mexican cinema. As World War II forced Hollywood film production into decline, Mexico – whose involvement in the conflict was more limited than the US – saw a prolific period of artistic development. Movie studios, such as Films Mundiales, opened in Mexico City, making it the film capital of Latin America at the time.

Lasting through to the 1950s, the era produced some of Mexico's most iconic films, created by directors like Emilio Fernández and Roberto Gavaldón. The latter's *Rosauro Castro* (1950) pushed boundaries by experimenting with film noir through dramatic backlighting and the use of intricate spaces. This period also introduced the world to some of the country's greatest movie stars, including María Félix, who starred in the Mexican romance *Maclovia* (1948); Dolores del Río, the lead in the epic historical drama *The Soldiers of Pancho Villa* (1959); and Pedro Infante, a Mexican ranchera singer who appeared in *Los tres huastecos* (1948), a comedy-drama that revolves around the lives of three very different brothers. These entertaining movies helped bring their leading actors – and Mexican cinema itself – into the limelight.

Above Movie star María Félix, pictured here in a 1950s film

Left Pedro Armendáriz in *Rosauro Castro*

MOVIES THAT MATTER

Cinema in Mexico wasn't just about entertainment, however. From the earliest days of the Mexican movie industry, its film-makers have rarely shied away from tackling difficult subject matter, confronting viewers with some of the most challenging issues facing Mexico. The country's turbulent 20th-century history – including a bloody revolution and the rise of a dictatorial one-party state – provided ample inspiration to local film-makers, who used their movies as a means to process the tumult, both for themselves and their viewers. The revolution in particular ignited Mexican cinema's penchant for the political, with the popular trilogy of 1930s films by pioneering director Fernando de Fuentes taking a critical look at the revolution itself.

MEXICAN MOVIE STARS

Dolores del Río
Regarded as the first major Latin American actress to break into Hollywood, del Río was a mainstay in Mexico's Golden Age, appearing in the iconic film *María Candelaria*.

Salma Hayek
Nominated for a Best Actress Oscar for her portrayal of artist Frida Kahlo in the film *Frida*, Salma Hayek is from the Mexican state of Veracruz.

Gael García Bernal
Hailing from the city of Guadalajara, García Bernal found mainstream success with his role in Iñárritu's film *Amores perros* (Love's a Bitch).

Diego Luna
Along with García Bernal, Luna starred in Cuarón's *Y tu mamá también* (And Your Mother Too) and has recently appeared in the *Star Wars* franchise.

Other directors sought to examine the country that emerged from these events. Their films became a vital lens through which issues like poverty and urban decay could be analyzed, often in unlikely genres such as film noir. Iconic films of the period include Luis Buñuel's *Los olvidados* (The Forgotten Ones, 1950), an unflinching look at poverty in Mexico, and *Distinto Amanecer* (Another Dawn, 1943) by Julio Bracho, where the crime-infested Mexico City becomes a central shadowy character in the film. Many of these films resonated with the Mexican public, becoming box office hits at home, and were critically acclaimed abroad.

Although the state began to exert greater influence over the industry in the 1970s, Mexican film-makers continued to tackle challenging issues. The brutal student massacre at Tlatelolco in 1968, for instance, was chronicled in the 1989 film *Rojo Amanecer* (Red Dawn); a box-office hit, it sparked heated discussion in Mexico, despite an attempt at government censorship. The feminist collective Cine Mujer, led by film-makers such as María Novaro and Maricarmen de Lara, also engaged with the turbulent political discourse of the time but from a decidedly feminist perspective.

NEW MEXICAN CINEMA

After a series of economic crises in the 1980s and early 1990s sent Mexican cinema into a downward spiral, the 1990s saw a film-making revival. This was partly down to greater government funding for Mexico's film industry and partly to a new wave of Mexican directors, who began to attract Hollywood's attention with films like *Como agua para chocolate* (Like Water for Chocolate). Directed by Alfonso Arau and released in 1992, this magical realist film – based

on a bestselling book – became a critical and commercial hit in Mexico and across the border. At the time, it was the highest-grossing foreign film in US history.

It was also during this period that a trio of film-makers emerged and transformed Mexican cinema forever: Alfonso Cuarón, Alejandro González Iñárritu and Guillermo del Toro. Together, the "three amigos", as they became known, helped usher in what is known as the *Nuevo Cine Mexicano* (New Mexican Cinema). Influenced by previous Mexican film-makers, they made gritty, realist films that focused on major contemporary themes in Mexican society and culture, including class division, violence, poverty and sexuality. These film-makers, who have since become Hollywood mainstays, received critical success in Mexico and around the world: Iñárritu's *Amores*

Above A scene from *Y tu mamá también*

Left *Identifying Features*, Fernanda Valadez's debut film

perros (Love's a Bitch) was nominated for Best Foreign Language Film at the Academy Awards in 2000, while Cuarón's *Y tu mamá también* (And Your Mother Too) received a Best Original Screenplay nod two years later. And in 2018, Del Toro's *The Shape of Water*, a mix of traditional Mexican folk horror and fantasy, nabbed 13 Academy Award nominations.

DEFYING THE STATUS QUO

Today, Mexican film-makers continue to tackle pressing problems affecting Mexican society, including drugs and corruption. Recent movies have captured the national imagination, including 2010's *El Infierno* (Hell) – a black comedy on the futility of the drug war and the chaos and corruption drug trafficking brings –

and the award-winning *Identifying Features* (2020), a poignant film about a mother searching for her lost migrant son. Directed by Fernanda Valadez, the latter is an example of a rise in films that centre on women protagonists and a female perspective – something that has been largely lacking in Mexico's male-dominated movie industry. Many of these female-led films have been critically acclaimed, with *Prayers for The Stolen*, a 2021 movie by Mexican-Salvadoran film-maker Tatiana Huezo, shortlisted for Best Foreign Language Film at the Academy Awards. Such movies are a clear indication that Mexican cinema will continue to do what it has always done – push boundaries, tackle difficult issues and challenge the status quo.

ICONIC FILMS

A global cinema powerhouse, Mexico has produced dozens of iconic films. With moving stories, extraordinary film-making and thrilling performances, these are some of Mexico's most ground-breaking movies.

MARÍA CANDELARIA (1943)

One of the most iconic films of Mexico's Golden Age, Emilio Fernández's 1943 film starred Pedro Armendáriz and Dolores del Río as an Indigenous couple struggling through a series of misfortunes in the community of Xochimilco. The first Latin American film to win the top prize at the Cannes Film Festival in France, the movie was one of the earliest to represent Indigenous Mexicans in a dignified light, although critics have since noted the portrayal as overly simplistic and idealized.

MACARIO (1960)

The first Mexican movie to be nominated for the Academy Awards' Best Foreign Language Film, *Macario* tells the story of a poor peasant and his encounter with Death personified. A supernatural drama, the film (directed by Roberto Gavaldón) stars legendary actor Ignacio López Tarso in a fantasy folktale which touches on several themes significant to Mexican culture, including an ambivalent and even comic relationship with death. It's widely regarded as one of Mexico's greatest films.

AMORES PERROS (2000)

Directed by Alejandro González Iñárritu and starring a young Gael García Bernal, *Amores perros* (Love's a Bitch) is a touchstone of the *Nuevo Cine Mexicano* (New Mexican Cinema). A gritty and often violent film, it tells the story of three strangers whose lives collide in a Mexico City car crash. The debut feature introduced the world to Iñárritu's signature multilayered narrative style and laid the foundation for what became a second Golden Age for Mexican film-making.

CARMÍN TROPICAL (2014)

As Mexico's film industry has become increasingly diverse, film-makers have sought to represent a broader range of stories. Rigoberto Perezcano's *Carmín Tropical* looks at the Indigenous *muxe* community from Oaxaca state, people who are born male but adopt female dress and societal roles. In the film, a young *muxe* travels back to her village in Oaxaca to investigate the death of one of her friends. A top prize-winner at the Morelia Film Festival, *Carmín Tropical* touches on issues of gender, sexuality and Indigenous culture.

ROMA (2018)

One of the most lauded Mexican films of recent years, Alfonso Cuarón's black-and-white epic provides a brilliant insight into the modern Mexican nation. Set in the Roma neighbourhood of Mexico City in the 1970s, the film follows an Indigenous woman named Cleo who works as a housekeeper for a middle-class Mexican family. Examining issues of class and race as well as documenting the political repression of the period, *Roma* took home three Oscars, including Best Foreign Language Film – a first for a Mexican movie.

1 Dolores del Río and Pedro Armendáriz in *María Candelaria*

2 A poster for *Macario*

3 *Amores perros*, starring Gael García Bernal

4 A scene from *Carmín Tropical*

5 Alfonso Cuarón's *Roma*

MACARIO

Starring
IGNACIO LOPEZ TARSO ★ PINA PELLICER

STORY   PHOTOGRAPHY   DIRECTION
BRUNO TRAVEN   ★   GABRIEL FIGUEROA   ★   ROBERTO GAVALDON

▶ BEST FOREIGN FILM NOMINEE
33rd ANNUAL ACADEMY AWARDS

SPECIAL AWARD   ★   BEST ACTOR
CANNES FILM FESTIVAL   SAN FRANCISCO FILM FESTIVAL

THE TV LANDSCAPE

Mexicans have been tuning in to their TVs for over 70 years, whether to catch up on the news, watch a football match or escape via one of the country's iconic telenovelas.

On 31 August 1950, Mexico's inaugural commercial television company began its first broadcast: the transmission of a speech by the Mexican president. Over the next decade, several other companies were set up but, due to a lack of advertising funding, were quickly merged into one single operation, Televisa. This company, run by the Azcárraga family, held a virtual monopoly over broadcasting during the rest of the 20th century. Popular programmes included sports, telenovelas (soap operas) and newscasts.

The end of the 20th and start of the 21st centuries saw a loosening of this monopoly, with two other television companies – TV Azteca and Imagen Television – established. However, the programmes on offer stayed largely the same as before, with telenovelas in particular as popular as ever.

THE TELENOVELA
No genre defines Mexican TV quite like the telenovela. These shows offer relatable, albeit melodramatic, accounts of daily life, with ordinary people falling in and out of love, navigating money troubles and family relationships, and pursuing their careers. Favourite plotlines include finding long-lost family members and a hapless protagonist falling in love with a rich or powerful suitor; the latter is a potential nod to the country's desire for upward mobility.

Beginning life in the 1930s as *radio-novelas*, these shows made the leap to the small screen in the 1950s. The first Mexican telenovela, *Senda prohibida* (Forbidden Path), was broadcast to great success in 1958. The format continued to be popular over the following decades, with many families sitting down to watch the shows together on weekday evenings. And they remain in-demand to this day: four out of five of the most-viewed programmes in Mexico are telenovelas, with shows like *Vencer* (Overcoming) commonly reaching millions of viewers.

STREAMING SUCCESS
Today, TV still plays a big role in entertaining Mexicans, with many owning a box. Yet online streaming services are growing in popularity, with around 12 million people now subscribed to one option or another.

The rise of such services has led to a boom in Mexican TV production, with companies like Netflix and Apple TV keen to cash in on the country's penchant for quality TV. Part of this growth has

Above A telenovela being filmed in Mexico City

been driven by more global interests, such as the world's fascination with narco culture. Series like *Narcos Mexico* have become international hits, particularly across Latin America and the US, spawning English-language iterations in their wake. While popular, these shows have strengthened both the narco stereotype within Mexico and global beliefs about Mexican daily life.

Mexican streaming shows encompass many other genres, too, from thrillers such as *Triptych* and mystery dramas like *La venganza de las juanas* (The Five Juanas), to the black comedy *La casa de las flores* (The House of Flowers). And, of course, telenovelas have their place: *Senda prohibida* was rebooted by Vix, an online streaming service, in 2023.

Narco Culture on TV

The success of Mexican productions such as *Narcos Mexico* and *El Chapo* has raised broader questions about the somewhat positive portrayal of narco culture on TV. Some shows tend to portray cartel bosses as visionary underdogs navigating a hostile society, fuelling the stereotype of the benevolent drug lord. However, this depiction jars with many of those living alongside the cartels, and the violence and corruption that they often sow. It's created an ongoing debate about the ethics of the shows.

POPULaR TV SHOWS

Telenovelas rule the roost when it comes to popularity, with many reaching vast audiences. Yet Mexican TV encompasses more than melodrama, with reality shows and saint-inspired dramas also big hits.

LA CASA DE LOS FAMOSOS

Part of the global *Big Brother* franchise, *La casa de los famosos México* (The Celebrities' House Mexico) became the most-watched Mexican reality TV show in 2023. It also saw the most engagement in Mexico's TV history, with 133 million votes cast by fans for their favourite celebrities. The show revealed increasingly progressive attitudes, too, with the Mexican public voting a transgender woman, Wendy Guevara, the winner.

VENCER

Kicking off in 2020, this telenovela series sees each of its standalone seasons explore a different feeling or emotion – such as fear or heartbreak – through the lives of four different women. The show hasn't been afraid to discuss taboo topics, which are often avoided by more traditionally conservative telenovelas. For instance *Vencer la culpa* (Overcoming Guilt), the fifth instalment of the franchise, touches on such subjects as divorce, sexually transmitted diseases and gender diversity.

ACAPULCO

Following the rags-to-riches story of a wealthy Mexican businessman, this feel-good comedy hops between modern-day Malibu and 1980s Acapulco, a resort town on Mexico's Pacific coast. While it draws on the country's beloved telenovelas – especially via somewhat melodramatic storylines – *Acapulco* is a new sort of show, one that can appeal to both global and Mexican audiences. Why? For one thing, it's bilingual, with its Mexican actors switching between Spanish and English; for another, it's got a high production value, thanks to streaming giant Apple TV – something that also makes it more accessible to a global audience.

TIERRA DE ESPERANZA

One of the most popular telenovelas of the early 2020s, *Tierra de esperanza* (Land of Hope) tells the story of a businesswoman who takes over her family's hacienda. Many of the usual telenovela themes are touched on, including a blossoming love-hate romance between the two lead characters. Produced by TelevisaUnivision, a Mexican-American company, the show was based on the Spanish-language American soap opera *La tormenta* (The Storm, 2005).

LA ROSA DE GUADALUPE

Few Catholic figures are revered more in Mexico than the Virgin of Guadalupe *(p66)*. It's unsurprising, then, that this TV show dedicated to her divine ways is so popular. Since it began in 2008, it's clocked up 15 seasons and huge ratings, especially among families, who crowd round the TV to watch come evening. Each episode focuses on someone going through a difficult time in their lives and how they ask for help from the Virgin – who invariably solves the problems with miraculous means.

1 A presenter on *La casa de los famosos México*

2 The main stars of *Vencer la culpa*

3 Welcoming guests to Las Colinas, the upscale resort featured in *Acapulco*

4 A scene from *Tierra de esperanza*

5 A poster advertising *La rosa de Guadalupe*

CReative COMEDY

Mexico's unique humour imbues many aspects of the country's culture. When life is at its darkest, comedy is a guiding light – and not even death is safe from the country's jokes.

Comedy in Mexico is multifaceted. Sometimes it's used as a way to cope with traumatic social, political and personal events, while at other points it becomes a way to challenge those in power. And most of all? It's simply an opportunity to enjoy a good laugh.

A DARK SENSE OF HUMOUR

"Only in Mexico is death an occasion for laughter." So says a reveller at the Day of the Dead celebrations in John Huston's film *Under the Volcano* (1984). Few countries have as many jocular euphemisms for death – "she hung up her tennis shoes", "he stretched out his leg", to name just two. Such an approach captures the Mexican willingness to use comedy in dark times, whether it's in reference to cartel killings or government corruption. For many Mexicans, finding the humour in such situations is by no means dismissing the horror of such events; instead, it acts as a form of cathartic release, especially when it comes to ongoing societal problems that can at times feel overwhelming.

One of Mexico's best-known comedians, Víctor Trujillo became famous for his use of dark humour, especially through his controversial comic persona "Brozo, the Dark Clown". This bitter, cynical and often politically incorrect character used acidic, vulgar humour to comment on Mexico's social and political reality; mocking presidents and making jokes about electoral fraud were regular go-tos. Such dark humour has been a means by which comedians can both hold those in power to account and educate the population.

THE POWER OF SATIRE

The very same could be said of satire, another tool in the arsenal of Mexican comedy. The country's satirical press has played a role in political struggles since the second half of the 19th century. Around the start of the 20th, newspapers such as *El Hijo del Ahuizote* published a variety of withering political cartoons, and were key to spreading revolutionary fervour.

Mexico's most famous satirical cartoonist was José Guadalupe Posada (1852–1913), who created the Day of the Dead symbol La Catrina (*p198*). His

engravings and illustrations paved the way for future political artists, whose work uses humour to attack hypocrisy. Today, cartoonists like Mexican-American Lalo Alcaraz continue to scrutinize contemporary issues through comic art, ridiculing things like migration policies and caricaturing political figures such as Donald Trump.

JUST FOR LAUGHS

Yet Mexican comedy doesn't always have a dark, more serious bent. Many everyday jokes revolve around an affectionate mocking between friends that often involves the *albur*, a double entendre (*p55*), or some other form of wordplay with sexual connotations. It's such a central part of Mexican comic culture that an annual competition is hosted to crown the best *alburero*. Yet this sort of playful teasing is reserved for friends only, with such double entendres seen as inappropriate for family conversations.

Comedy star Mario Moreno (1911–1993), better known as Cantinflas, excelled at wordplay during the mid-20th century. Often playing the *pelado* role (a rude, uneducated urban "slum dweller" from Mexico City), his everyman persona and quick-talking wit appealed to audiences both within Mexico and abroad. He was so influential that the verb *cantinflear* was coined, meaning to speak incongruously without saying anything.

Quick-witted wordplay was also used by Germán Valdés (1915–1973), better known as Tin-Tan. A contemporary of Cantinflas, he perfected the art and aesthetic of *pachuco*, which involved using "Spanglish" slang (commonly spoken on the Mexican border) and wearing exaggerated zoot suits. Chaplin-esque choreographed slapstick was a hallmark of his films, as it was for those featuring Cantinflas – in fact, Charlie Chaplin described the latter as "the greatest comedian alive".

Above Tin-Tan *(right)* in a 1950s comedy-romance

THE SPORTING LIFE

Whether played on horseback, in the wrestling ring or on a football pitch, sport unites Mexicans in shared camaraderie. For many, sport is more than just a game: it's a way of life.

In Mexican sporting arenas, victory isn't always the be all and end all. The honour and ceremony of participation often mean more than striving for a win, while the country's love of the underdog is reflected in its sporting heroes. Though Mexico's sports scene has changed drastically due to urbanization, nothing unites the country like the communal spectacle of a game.

THE NATIONAL SPORT

If any sport highlights the importance of ceremony in Mexico, it's *charrería*. The *charrería* sees local charros (cowboys) perform an array of impressive equestrian activities, showcasing their talents across 10 different *suertes* (games). These include the roping of a horse's feet, during which a lasso is used to bind the hind legs of a moving horse, and the riding of the bull, when a charro will attempt to stay on a bucking bull for as long as possible. Competitors are judged on their style, poise and execution.

Right A Mexican charro (cowboy) practising lassoing ahead of a *charrería*

Much like the American rodeo, *charrería* dates to the arrival of Spanish conquistadors, who introduced horses to the country. Across Mexico's rural haciendas, horses became integral to the local economy, both as livestock to be traded and as a means of simplifying agricultural labour. Private competitions

Those Who Run Fast

The Rarámuri, an Indigenous people who live in the mountains of Mexico's Sierra Madre Occidental, have captivated the world's imagination with their ability to run extremely long distances. Members of this community – whose name means "those who run fast" – can jog hundreds of kilometres over several days. Their remarkable athletic feats are due to a combination of lifestyle, culture and achievement: for years they would hunt prey over long distances in high altitudes.

showcasing derring-do began between ranch hands, and in the 1930s the newly created National Charro Association launched a drive to formalize the sport, with events held in arenas in Mexico City. The sport was imbued with a sense of heroism during the Golden Age of Mexican cinema, when stars like Pedro Infante glamorized the charro lifestyle on screen. To this day, charros are rarely paid for their participation; they do it for the honour and tradition of the sport.

For much of *charrería*'s history, this sense of honour was seen as exclusively masculine, with women barred from competing. However, in 1972, Ana María Zermeño – the granddaughter of influential *charrería* promoters, better known by her sporting name La Prieta – founded a charro association called Las Alteñitas de Guadalajara. The association fought hard for the participation of *escaramuza* (female rodeo riders) in *charrería*, helping to transform the perception of women in the sport. Today, one of the official *suertes* – also known as the *escaramuza* – is performed by women only.

While the latter half of the 20th century saw the sport's popularity decline, largely due to mass urbanization, *charrería* remains a vital example of Mexican tradition, with many still participating across the country.

STORIES FROM MEXICO

As a *charro*, it is with great pride that I represent a culture, an identity and a country. Just as you might get goosebumps from listening to mariachi, being a *charro* evokes the same intense emotions.

Charrería is an integral part of the daily routine for many Mexicans in rural areas; it's a deeply ingrained habit and a cherished tradition. My father, brothers and children all proudly carry the title of *charros*, and my sisters are *escaramuzas*.

Charrería will not be lost anytime soon, especially because our children love the sport; they enjoy the fact that it's high-intensity and that it links them to nature. Plus, there are many youth competitions run by the Mexican Federation of Charrería. *Charrería* will continue to be Mexico's national sport, as it preserves Mexican equestrian traditions and is a symbol of Mexican pride.

José Julio Villaseñor, member of the Mexican Federation of Charrería, Baja California

Above A *luchador* takes a flying jump at his competitors

Left Performing in the *escaramuza*

THE MASKED HEROES

While *charrería* never really became a televised sport, it was a different story for lucha libre. A form of freestyle wrestling, this sport sees *luchadores* (wrestlers) take to the ring in masks (*p150*), using highly stylized manoeuvres, including acrobatic flying kicks and jumps, to fight their foes. Each choreographed match has a dramatic narrative that pits the *rudos* (villains) against the *técnicos* (heroes). While the winners may be predetermined, that doesn't stop the crowds from cheering with excitement, thanks to the theatre of the sport.

Lucha libre was born in 1922, when Salvador Lutteroth Gonzales, partly inspired by Greco-Roman wrestling, set up the Empresa Mexicana de Lucha Libre (Mexican Wrestling Company) in Mexico City. It wasn't until the 1950s and 1960s, however, that the sport hit the mainstream, with matches first broadcast on TV. These televised events turned *luchadores* into household names, with stars such as El Santo appearing in blockbuster films like *El Santo Contra los zombies* (1961). While matches still draw large TV audiences, today's biggest wrestling league (the AAA) makes most of its revenue from ticket sales and sponsorship, with matches attracting crowds of up to 17,000 spectators.

As lucha libre has grown in popularity, it's also become more inclusive. In the 20th century, the sport was inextricably linked to the "macho" characteristics of strength, force and courage; as a result,

it wasn't seen as a suitable pastime for women, who were thought of as passive and fragile. While some women took part in the sport during the 1920s and 1930s, the next few decades saw them forced to the fringes, with a full ban on women participating enacted in 1954. Yet things began to change in the 1990s, with more *luchadoras* (female wrestlers) taking to the ring. And while women's leagues can't quite compete with the popularity of the men's, the success of *luchadoras* like Lady Apache have made the sport far more welcoming than it once was.

Macho attitudes in the ring also made it difficult for gay *luchadores*. While flamboyantly camp wrestlers, known as *exóticos*, have participated since the 1940s, none were openly gay. This changed in 1987, when Saúl Armendáriz became the first *luchador* to proudly announce his homosexuality. Known as "Cassandro" in the ring, he initially faced prejudice before going on to achieve huge celebrity and success. *Cassandro*, a film about his life and the wider culture of *exóticos*, was released in 2023.

GLOBAL GAMES

As well as its homegrown offerings, Mexico makes space for sports from around the globe. Some of these are relatively obscure: *pelota vasca*, similar to squash or racquetball, is a popular

Above Statue of a *pelota vasca* player in Baja California

Right Striker Hugo Sánchez during a match with Norway

recreational sport in Mexico that originated in Spain's Basque country. The sport arrived in the early 20th century with Basque migrants, and now has various iterations; it can be played with the hands, with a wooden bat or a racket.

Some Mexican-adopted sports, however, are known the world over; the country's three favourites are football, baseball and boxing. These games have produced Mexico's foremost sporting idols: the prolific goal-scoring footballer Hugo Sánchez, the baseball pitcher Fernando Valenzuela and the boxer Julio César Chávez. In 1990, the latter became a national legend when he came back from a sure defeat to beat his opponent with only five seconds left in the fight.

Of the three, football is the most popular and is the most televised sporting event in Mexico. Since it became a professional sport in the country in 1943, its top tier, Liga MX, has been one of the most watched football leagues in the Americas, with viewing figures rising both domestically and internationally. While league football is getting bigger, the Mexican people's true passion is El Tri (the national team). Every time the team plays in a championship – especially the World Cup – millions of Mexicans dream, celebrate and suffer together, following the fortunes of their beloved players. And although results on the world stage have never been great, football remains a great unifying force in the country. When gathered around the TV or huddled together in the stadium, fans are not expecting victory: it's the joy of playing together that means most.

The MÁSCARAS of LUCHA LIBRE

In lucha libre, the *máscara* (mask) is far more than a costume. Covering the whole head – with gaps for the eyes, nose and mouth – each mask acts as a symbol of a *luchador*'s honour, prestige and unique identity. It also helps give a wrestler a sense of mystery, and separates their public persona from their private life.

While numerous origin stories of the *máscara* circulate, it's claimed that American wrestler Corbin James Massey was the first to wear one when he came to compete in Mexico in 1933. Covered by a simple black mask, La Maravilla Enmascarada (The Masked Marvel), as he was known, caught the Mexican public's attention. Such disguise quickly became ubiquitous, with other wrestlers donning masks. Among them was El Santo, who became one of Mexico's most famous *luchadores*. His silver mask, which he was buried in, is still one of the most recognizable in the sport. Others include the blue-and-silver headgear of the Blue Demon (one of El Santo's main rivals) and the crown-branded mask of Rey Mysterio, another iconic *luchador*. While some masks are kept simple, others are more elaborate, including horned and bejewelled offerings.

Fun they may be, but mask-wearing is bound by strict conventions and traditions. Forced removal of a wrestler's mask during a fight will lead to disqualification, while "mask vs mask" battles involve a wager: whoever loses will be unmasked, and publicly stripped of their honour. In families where wrestling stretches through the generations, fathers even pass on the design of their mask to their sons – and with it their public prestige and legacy.

Dance styles

On a dance floor, at a fiesta or in a theatre: dance is all around in Mexico. And it's more than just moving to music. Running the gamut from ballet to *la bamba*, dance styles in Mexico show off this country's varied past.

By incorporating influences from Europe, Africa and the Caribbean, not forgetting Indigenous traditions, Mexico has forged a dynamic dance scene. So whether it's *la danza Azteca* or *jarabe tapatío*, one thing is clear: Mexicans love to dance.

INDIGENOUS IDENTITIES

For Indigenous cultures, dance was a central form of religious expression. Ritualized movement involving elaborate costumes and heavy percussion was used to pay homage to gods and to connect with revered ancestors. Aztec dancers would move in a state of euphoria, while drummers hammered out the beat on a *huehuetl* (a decorated drum made from a hollowed-out tree trunk). For many Aztec groups, the *huehuetl* was seen as the embodiment of a community's ancestors, and dancing to its beat created a vital channel between past and present.

Following colonization, Indigenous dance took on a political significance. In Tlaxcala, the base of Hernán Cortés's *(p38)* invading forces, elaborately choreographed routines were used to dramatize the colonial struggle. The Tlaxcalans wore colourful headdresses and garish masks representing European features to depict clashes between colonizers and Indigenous communities. The display is still practised during the annual Tlaxcalan carnival.

Today, Aztec dance (referred to as *la danza Azteca*) is an enduring part of Mexico's cultural landscape. Aztec dance troupes perform everywhere from markets to festivals; their popularity is not simply a tourist spectacle, but is part of a genuine celebration of Indigenous heritage. Descendants of the Aztecs aren't the only Indigenous group in Mexico to celebrate their rich culture of dance, with other communities such as the Purepecha *(p155)* performing traditional *danzas* that honour their heritage.

GLOBAL RHYTHMS

European styles like flamenco poured into port cities, including Veracruz, following Mexico's colonization. These European dances were soon followed by Caribbean and African influences, brought along with the transatlantic slave trade. Veracruz's emblematic *la bamba* dance features Cuban and African elements merged with flamenco-esque movements, while Guadalajara's energetic *jarabe tapatío*, a courtship dance, took influence from Spanish styles such as *fandangos* and *seguidillas*. In fact, many of Mexico's

most iconic dances originate beyond the country's borders: the slow, pensive and wistful movements of *danzón* arrived from Cuba in the late 19th century and the folk dance known as *cumbia* originated in Colombia.

Thanks to global influences, more formalized approaches have also become part of Mexican dance – something best showcased by the Ballet Folklórico de México. Also known as Ballet Folklórico de Amalia Hernández – in honour of its eponymous founder – this revered dance company strives to document Mexico's varied folk dance styles, combining these with more formalized choreography, techniques and costumes. The Folklórico puts on seasonal performances at the Palacio de Bellas Artes in Mexico City, where they have been in residence for more than 60 years.

Amalia Hernández

Amalia Hernández (1917–2000) is regarded as the woman who brought Mexican dance and music to the world. Born in Mexico City, she began dancing as a child and went on to study at the National School of Dance. Dissatisfied by the focus on modern and European styles, she founded the Ballet Folklórico de México in 1952, which placed a strong focus on traditional Mexican forms of dance. She choreographed over 60 dances in her lifetime, typically blending Indigenous and regional influences with modern techniques.

ON THE MAP

TYPES OF DANCE

Mexico is awash with different dance styles, which can vary from state to state, city to city and even village to village. Many have their roots in the country's Indigenous peoples and heritage, while others are an amalgamation or evolution of styles from such places as Europe and Africa. This map showcases a small selection of the dances found across Mexico.

In **Sonora** state, the *danza del venado* portrays a traditional Yaqui and Mayo deer hunt. It's led by "the deer", a near-blindfolded dancer who wears a taxidermied deer head; this dancer imitates the creature's movements, while being pursued by "the hunters", known as *pascolas*. The dance is also practised in Sinaloa.

Hailing from **Nayarit**, the *danza de los machetes* sees dancers – who are sometimes blindfolded – slice machetes through the air, before clanging them together. It's all part of a complexly choreographed "courting ritual", with simply clad male dancers hoping to win favour with their elegant female counterparts.

The state of **Queretaro**'s *danza de los concheros* incorporates incense, conch shells and feathered headdresses. The dance combines Indigenous elements with Christian imagery and European instruments, depicting a transition from Indigenous gods to Catholic worship.

Performed by Afro-Mexican communities in **Oaxaca**, the *danza de los diablos* pays homage to an African god, Ruja; over time, the dance merged with Mexican spiritual traditions, and today is performed around the Day of the Dead. The dance, which also takes place in Guerrero, involves rhythmic foot stomping, with each of the dancers wearing a bearded mask.

Originating in Jarácuaro, **Michoacán**, the *danza de los viejitos* was once performed by Purepecha *petámunis* (elders) every quarter to mark the seasons. It's now a humorous ritual staged on major holidays, in which four participants – all dressed as old men carrying walking sticks – try to keep up with an ever-increasing rhythm.

CREATIVE MEXICO

Think of Mexican art and it's probably Frida Kahlo's iconic works that first spring to mind. This unparalleled artist used her paintings to tell not just her own story, but that of Mexico itself. And she's not the only one. Mexicans have long used art as a way to convey a sense of both identity and community, from Indigenous artisans using traditional crafts to honour their heritage to the 20th-century muralists who forged a modern Mexican identity in their paintings. Architecture, too, has played a role, tracing the history of Mexico through the ages and showcasing the evolving beliefs of Mexicans over time. Today's creators show no signs of stopping, with a new generation of writers, artists and architects thinking up innovative ways to write Mexico's ever-evolving story.

Mexican Art Through the Ages

A testament to the cultural wealth of the nation, Mexican art weaves together Indigenous traditions, Spanish-era influences and revolutionary spirit.

Art has long been a channel for exploring and conveying identity and ideas in Mexico. Ancient civilizations such as the Olmecs and Aztecs depicted what was important to them, including the natural world, politics and religion. The colonial period, meanwhile, brought great transformation with the introduction of new ideas, materials and techniques from Europe. Following the Mexican Revolution, art in the country became an increasingly important means of establishing a unified sense of national identity, while also reflecting the country's complex cultural heritage, pressing political issues and changing global perspectives.

ANCIENT ART

The earliest examples of art from here come from the country's nomadic inhabitants, who left their mark on the walls of the caves they used for temporary shelter. Dating back as far as 10,000 BCE, these cave paintings depict human and animal figures, showing the practical concerns of hunting and gathering, as well as abstract designs which may reflect astronomical themes. With a shift to settled living around 2000 BCE, clay items began to be produced. Figurines depicting women with wide hips became very common, and may have been used in agricultural fertility rituals.

DEVELOPING FORMS

As civilizations developed so did their art, with remarkable sculptures, pottery and murals standing as evidence of the complex cultural systems of ancient Mexico. The Olmecs, for instance, carved colossal heads out of basalt boulders.

Above Mayan mural at the ancient city of Bonampak, Chiapas

Left Prehistoric rock paintings on the Baja California peninsula

These sculptures likely portrayed rulers, marking a transition to a hierarchical society and centralized form of governance around 1500 BCE. The 8th-century CE murals at the ancient Mayan site of Bonampak, meanwhile, show the rituals of courtly life, including processions, the reception of foreign dignitaries and acts of human sacrifice. The painters of these murals used a complex palette of pigments, including the striking "Mayan blue", an incredibly vibrant and durable colour made from a composite of plants and minerals.

The Aztecs of the 13th and 14th centuries practised similar art forms, as well as creating intricate pieces with feathers. A special class of artisans known as *amanteca* made headdresses, ceremonial shields and other decorative pieces using the plumes of a variety of birds, including highly prized iridescent quetzal tail feathers. As feathers represented celestial entities and were considered sacred, these items were mainly worn by the upper classes for ritual purposes – it was believed that those who donned them were converted into divine beings.

Drawing on techniques used by older Mesoamerican civilizations, the Aztecs also produced ceramics. These were handmade from red and orange clay,

Above Colourful
nearika tapestry made
out of wool

Above right The spire of
Iglesia de Santa
María Tonantzintla

open-fired and decorated using natural pigments. While some items were produced for everyday use by all levels of society, such as pots for cooking beans or soaking maize kernels overnight, other, more elaborate items were fashioned for use in rituals, such as incense burners and funerary urns.

FUSION OF STYLES

Following the arrival of the Spanish in the 16th century, there was a fusion of European and Indigenous art, leading to the development of a new style: Tequitqui. Local Indigenous artisans began to decorate the new *conventos* and churches that were established by Spanish friars. Using traditional stone carving techniques, they blended Catholic themes with Indigenous symbols. These were often tied to natural themes, including agriculture, fertility, the seasons and the tree of life. The Iglesia de Santa María de Tonantzintla is an example of this style: built on the site of an earlier temple to the Aztec mother

whole communities would specialize in a certain type of craft, passing their knowledge down through generations over centuries – a practice that continues to this day. Indeed, the Wixáritari (or Huichol) of the Western Sierra Madre region have an ancestral tradition of making colourful tablets called *nearika* by pressing vibrant wool or beads into a layer of wax and resin to create intricate designs. Each piece is considered a prayer and an offering to the gods. In ancient times they were likely made with seeds, but now these pieces are fashioned from imported beads or wool.

CRAFTING A NATIONAL IDENTITY

After the Mexican Revolution in the early 20th century *(p40)*, muralism, a medium that drew on the country's artistic heritage, became prominent. Aiming to create a cohesive national identity following years of conflict, the

goddess Tonantzin, it's decorated with plaster figures of angels – many with dark skin – surrounded by colourful feathers and motifs of flowers, fruits and plants.

Over the next few centuries, local artisans also continued to produce traditional crafts and folk art that maintained strong ties to those pieces created by earlier Mesoamerican civilizations. As with Tequitqui, natural objects – including animals, plants and flowers – were major themes. These Mexican *artesanías* (handicrafts or folk art) were produced in a number of mediums, including embroidery and weavings, finely worked pottery, whimsical woodcarvings, and elaborate silver and gold jewellery *(p168)*. Often

Luz Jiménez

A Nahuatl speaker from a rural area, Luz Jiménez moved to Mexico City in the early 1920s and was soon in high demand as a model among artists who saw her as embodying an ideal of Indigenous beauty. Her image appears in murals and monuments throughout the city, but she also served as a consultant to linguists and ethnographers and left behind first-hand accounts of the Mexican Revolution and life in rural Mexico.

Mexican government commissioned artists, including Diego Rivera, David Alfaro Siqueiros and José Clemente Orozco – known as "The Big Three" – to paint the walls of public buildings, thereby kick-starting the Muralist Movement. Murals were the art form of choice for two main reasons: firstly, because they drew on a long heritage of Mesoamerican wall paintings and fostered a sense of continuity with the past. Secondly, because they were a truly accessible form of art: at the time, the majority of Mexicans were illiterate, but murals allowed the development of a clear artistic language that all could understand and enjoy.

The murals of this era celebrated the country's Indigenous heritage, glorified the ideals of the revolution and conveyed a sense of national pride. They went hand-in-hand with the development of *Mexicanidad* (essentially the essence of what it means to be Mexican), which was tied to a deep pride in the country's rich history. Some murals, such as Rivera's *The Great City of Tenochtitlán*, showcased this heritage, whereas others spoke to the largely socialist leanings of the muralists, with ordinary people, including workers and peasants, portrayed as heroes fighting for the future of Mexico. Many pieces also highlighted the country's complex social issues, a focus that continues with the new generation of muralists who are working today.

Above right Betsabeé Romero standing before *The Altar*, inspired by Mayan celebrations

Above left Rivera's *History of Mexico* mural at Mexico City's Palacio Nacional

CONTEMPORARY ART

Mexico's current artistic scene continues to reflect the country's complex cultural heritage, its social issues and its modern identity. Many contemporary Mexican artists are at the forefront of innovative and experimental practices, while still drawing inspiration from Indigenous roots. Betsabeé Romero and Demián Flores, for instance, incorporate Mesoamerican symbols and iconography into their art. Romero uses Mexico's traditional imagery to explore complex issues related to gender and migration. Flores, meanwhile, founded the Taller Gráfica Actual collective in the city of Oaxaca, to serve as a creative space for traditional graphic mediums such as lithography and etching, infused with contemporary designs. The artist's work not only celebrates Indigenous culture but also confronts issues of identity, colonization and the preservation of ancestral knowledge.

Teresa Margolles' art, meanwhile, shines a light on the violence and death that result from drug-related crime, poverty and political upheaval. She produces works that have a material connection to death, with many of her pieces imbued with physical traces of death such as blood-stained sheets, glass shards, bullets and used surgical threads.

Contemporary art is also thriving on the margins in Mexico City, with collectives of young creatives setting up small galleries away from the main art hubs. Small, temporary pop-up exhibition spaces explore everything from ecological decay to progressive urban infrastructure. With such a wealth of talent, it's clear that Mexico's artists will continue to flourish, creating pieces that define the modern nation.

MODERN MEXICAN ARTISTS

Miguel Calderón
Through photography, video, performance and music, Calderón explores dark themes with an ironic gaze, pointing to Mexico's corruption and violence.

Minerva Cuevas
Using brand logos and an assortment of familiar objects, Cuevas' work invites reflection on the structures that underlie social and economic systems.

Francisco Toledo
Blending folk traditions, Francisco Toledo made paintings, prints, photography and ceramics that depict a world populated by fantastical animals.

Pedro Reyes
Reyes seeks playful answers to social problems, often by subverting the use of everyday objects. In one of his projects, he transformed guns into various musical instruments.

Betsabeé Romero
Using recycled materials, Romero explores mobility, immigration, gender and the tensions between industrialized society and local Indigenous traditions in Mexico.

ICONIC MEXICAN ARTWORKS

Whether challenging viewers with their avant-garde styles or plainly portraying the plight of the working class, Mexico's extraordinary muralists and innovative painters have contributed greatly to the global art scene. These are just a few of the nation's many artistic touchstones from the 20th century.

EL HOMBRE CONTROLADOR DEL UNIVERSO (1934), DIEGO RIVERA

Diego Rivera is one of Mexico's most celebrated artists, and this huge mural shows why. Commissioned in 1932 by the American businessman John D Rockefeller, *Man, Controller of the Universe* depicts the common worker, surrounded by the competing ideological forces of capitalism and Communism. A Communist himself, Rivera included a portrait of Russian revolutionary Vladimir Lenin, which caused such distaste to the Rockefeller family that they had the original mural painted over. Rivera painted another version inside the Palacio de Bellas Artes in Mexico City, which can still be admired to this day.

AUTORRETRATO CON COLLAR DE ESPINAS Y COLIBRÍ (1940), FRIDA KAHLO

Now an icon of popular culture, for many years Frida Kahlo *(p166)* lived in the shadow of her more famous husband, Diego Rivera. But paintings like this one, also known as *Self-portrait with Necklace of Thorns and Hummingbird*, demonstrate why, in recent years, Kahlo has eclipsed Rivera in international renown. Painted after her divorce from Rivera, the piece is rife with suffering, particularly the collar of thorns slicing the artist's neck (echoing Christ's crown in a nod to Mexico's Catholic traditions) and the dead hummingbird (a messenger of love and good news in ancient Aztec culture). Like much of Kahlo's best work, the painting is a powerful synthesis of Mexican iconography and the artist's personal suffering.

ECHO OF A SCREAM (1937) DAVID ALFARO SIQUEIROS

Although known as one of Mexico's greatest muralists, Siqueiros *(p162)* also completed dozens of paintings, including this work from 1937. The work exemplifies Siqueiros' use of experimental materials and techniques, using wood instead of canvas and acrylic (or in this case enamel) instead of oil paints. The powerful work depicts a child in an agonized cry surrounded by a ravaged landscape.

TRES PERSONAJES (1970), RUFINO TAMAYO

One of Mexico's most important artists, Rufino Tamayo captures the mysticism of Mexican culture, while using techniques and styles from the European avant-garde. *Tres Personajes*, or *The Three Figures*, depicts a man, a woman and a third androgynous person in an abstract fashion, rendered in deep purple, ochre and yellow. With echoes of Cubism and Abstract Expressionism, Tamayo presents an image that is deeply evocative and compellingly ambiguous.

1 Rivera painting his mural in the hall of the Rockefeller Center, New York City

2 A detail of Kahlo's self-portrait, which features a hummingbird and a collar of thorns

3 *Echo of a Scream*, painted on wood

4 The striking, avant-garde *Tres Personajes*

FRIDA KAHLO

Mexico's pre-eminent painter and foremost cultural icon, Frida
Kahlo (1907–1954) was born and raised in the borough of
Coyoacán, on the outskirts of Mexico City. The artist was no
stranger to hardship: at age 6 she was bedridden for several
months with polio and in her teens suffered a near-fatal bus
accident. Her early adulthood, meanwhile, saw her embark on
a tumultuous relationship with Diego Rivera, who she met
through their work with the Mexican Communist Party.

These challenges, coupled with Kahlo's singular imagination,
would fuel her artistic vision. Her convention-defying work
consists mostly of self-portraits, which are rich in folkloric
Mexican symbolism. Portraits such as *The Two Fridas* (1939) and
The Broken Column (1944) explore dual European and
Indigenous identities, while celebrating female empowerment.
Her painting *Moses* (1945) is a vibrant kaleidoscope of feminist,
socialist and Aztec imagery, capturing the revolutionary spirit
of her work. Kahlo's remarkable output was produced in under
three decades: she died unexpectedly at the age of 47.

Few artists are now as globally celebrated and ubiquitous as
Frida Kahlo. Her image, as often seen on mugs and T-shirts as
on the walls of a gallery, has inspired a new generation, while
her portraits have become a beacon to the oppressed and
the marginalized. Some contemporary critics have observed
that the commodification of Kahlo's work has come at a cost
to other female artists, with their art eclipsed by Kahlo's
monumental brand. Even so, there's no getting away from the
power of her profile.

ARtiSaNaL CRafts

For thousands of years, Mexico's visionary artisans
have created exquisite handicrafts, using rare materials
and sophisticated techniques passed down through
the generations.

Mexico's varied handicrafts, or
artesanías, encompass a wide range
of influences, styles and colour palettes.
The broad term *artesanías* captures
the variety of the country's folk art,
indicating both functional goods –
including plates, textiles, glassware
and so forth – as well as decorative
items, such as wall hangings and sculptures. Whether designed to decorate
a house, denote rank or simply to
serve dinner, handicrafts have long
been an important part of Mexico's
artistic heritage.

EARLY CRAFTS

Mexico's tradition of folk art and
handicrafts dates back to the great
Mesoamerican civilizations. The potters
of the Olmec Empire developed early
techniques for firing clay, and earthen-
ware vessels featuring anthropomorphic
figures have been discovered in ancient
Olmec cities such as La Venta. Many of
their crafts, including clay effigies of
gods, were linked to spiritual practices,
while others, including jewellery of gold
and jade, were a recognition of status.

As an elite class developed in the
empire's city-states, demand for the
production of luxury crafts increased,
and a variety of intricate artifacts
sculpted from materials like jade
and obsidian have been discovered by
archaeologists across the Mesoamerican
region and beyond.

The ancient Mayans in southern
Mexico were adept sculptors, crafting
icons hewn from stone, wood, bone
and fired clay. During the flourishing
of the Mayan Empire, around 200 to
800 CE, rulers employed respected
artisans and stonemasons to decorate
royal buildings in vast city-states, often
with large stone figures of deities or
divine beings.

AZTEC ARTISANS

Artisanal crafts flourished under the
Aztec Empire in the 14th and 15th
centuries, with the development of
innovative new techniques and the
expansion of networks for trading.
Artisans and craftspeople including
potters, metal workers, weavers,
feather workers and scribes were
revered and known collectively as the
tolteca (they were named after the
earlier Toltec civilization, who the
Aztecs respected for their ingenuity).

Above left A potter moulding clay by hand

Above right A young girl with a traditional hand-woven shawl

The empire's craftspeople worked in large-scale workshops, producing fine works that were sold and exchanged through the flourishing trade system, particularly at sprawling markets surrounding the capital, Tenochtitlán (p36). Historical records show that textiles and fabrics were widely traded, with complex decorative pieces fetching high prices depending on the quality of their designs. Ceramics were also some of the empire's most prized handicrafts, with talented potters firing clay and moulding vessels, tools and even musical instruments by hand.

The best crafts were reserved for the empire's nobility. Nobles adorned themselves with feather capes and headdresses, as well as elaborate jewellery, including earrings, nose rings and bracelets. Jewellery was either carved from natural items, such as bone, wood or shell, or fashioned from precious metals and stones, including gold, jade and topaz. While these more refined items were reserved for the

Vida Nueva

Founded in 1994, the Vida Nueva women's weaving co-operative in Oaxaca supports women who are single, widowed, have absent migrant husbands or are survivors of domestic abuse. Located in Teotitlán del Valle, the co-operative makes and sells beautiful rugs using traditional weaving techniques and natural dyes, with the profits providing support to women who have little other resources. The organization also delivers local workshops on issues like domestic violence and alcoholism.

upper classes, other, less sophisticated forms of decoration were available to those of lower classes.

NEW TECHNIQUES

Many of Mexico's traditional crafts changed as new tools, products and techniques arrived from Europe throughout the 17th and 18th centuries. The introduction of the potter's wheel and open-top kilns facilitated a new age of ceramics. The now world-famous Talavera ceramics (p173) were carefully crafted in the state of Puebla, using European techniques but made of unique, rich volcanic clay that is perfect for complex pottery.

The Spanish also brought new techniques for working with metal: these approaches influenced

Indigenous people in the western state of Michoacán who have since become well known for their copperwork, creating pots, vases and cookware with intricate designs.

AN ARTISANAL REVIVAL

Despite the influence of US and Chinese manufacturing and imports in the 20th and 21st centuries, there is still a place for artisanal crafts in Mexico. In western and northern Mexico, for instance, the Wixáritari (or Huichol) create jewellery and giant sculptures in psychedelic colours from thousands of beads delicately woven or stuck together.

In Oaxaca state, the community of Teotitlán del Valle is known for its weaving, producing rugs and carpets in a variety of natural dyes – from ochre to indigo, terracotta to gold – based on old techniques and traditions. Weavers in fabric-rich states like Chiapas in southern Mexico, meanwhile, have become increasingly important to Mexico's fashion industry, with their use of organic fibres, natural dyes and centuries-old techniques providing inspiration for a sustainable future.

It's not just fashion that is being influenced by old artisanal techniques. The capital has become a global hub of contemporary art and design, with ateliers like Ewe Studio creating cutting-edge pieces of sculpture and furniture that pay homage to Mexico's traditions while pushing craftsmanship to new levels; these include vases inspired by ritualistic vessels or furniture pieces carved from black obsidian. While traditions are being adapted to make modern products, shoppers can still buy original handicrafts at the country's many craft markets, much like the Aztecs would have done centuries ago.

STORIES FROM MEXICO

I have been a jewellery maker for 13 years. As a teenager, I met people in the plaza of my hometown, who taught me how to make bracelets using thread. Later, I attended a jewellery workshop, and learned about the ancient origins of the practice. Today, I sell my pieces on the main street of Zipolite, in Oaxaca state.

In pre-colonial Mexico, jewellery was used to denote rank, with ancient cultures using precious stones and feathers as well as materials like gold. Every piece had its meaning. Jewellery was made to be worn by nobles and priests or given as offerings to the gods.

These ancient cultures continue to inspire my work, which combines metals and precious stones as well as feathers and other objects. In particular, the Mexica and Zapotec cultures constantly inspire me. I'm also inspired by nature.

But my favourite part about making jewellery is that no two pieces are the same: I like that everything is unique.

Sandra Irán Pradel Gutiérrez, Milpa Alta

ON THE MAP

TRADITIONAL CRAFTS

Mexico's talented craftspeople are the custodians of rare techniques, closely guarding methods that have been finessed over generations. Their use of unique, local resources means the country's crafts vary significantly from region to region; some might be bought and sold worldwide, but they owe their existence to a single town or village. Here are some of the most notable local handicrafts from across Mexico.

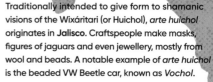

Traditionally intended to give form to shamanic visions of the Wixáritari (or Huichol), *arte huichol* originates in **Jalisco**. Craftspeople make masks, figures of jaguars and even jewellery, mostly from wool and beads. A notable example of *arte huichol* is the beaded VW Beetle car, known as *Vochol*.

It's the pre-firing, quartz-stone polishing process that gives *barro negro* ("black clay"), from **Oaxaca** state, its colour and high-shine finish. The delicate cutouts and reliefs also set this fine style of pottery apart. The works are traditionally produced in the town of San Bartolo Coyotepec.

An artisanal process passed down since Mesoamerican times, the creation of copper goods in the town of Santa Clara del Cobre, **Michoacán** endures to this day. Traditionally hand moulded, each piece – typically kitchen wares such as pots, pans and cups – is as unique as the last.

Commonly associated with the town of Metepec, **State of Mexico**, *árboles de la vida* ("Trees of Life") are highly decorative ceramic ornaments often gifted at weddings. Although modern examples sometimes narrate personal life stories, or centre on specific themes, most tend towards depicting the religious.

Primarily blue and white tones mark out **Pueblo's** Talavera designs – including tiles, teapots and dishes – from other ceramics. Still made using arduous processes (including purifying two types of clay), Talavera pottery is considered of Intangible Cultural Heritage by UNESCO.

ALEBRIJES

The small, predominantly wooden animal sculptures known as *alebrijes* are among Mexico's most emblematic (and popular) styles of folk art. Vividly coloured, intricately hand-painted and whimsical in nature, they depict creatures both real and fantastical. But contrary to what the Disney film *Coco* (2017) may have you believe, they're not "spirit guides", and only date to the early 20th century.

Invented by Mexico City *cartonero* (paper craftsperson) Pablo Linares back in 1936, *alebrijes* were born – or so the popular tale goes – of a fever dream, during which the artist hallucinated fantastical beings chanting a "nonsense" word: *alebrije*. Recovered, he re-created the mishmashed creatures in papier-mâché, using wire to shape the base, cardboard to add bulk and newspaper to create the form, before painting them with vivid colours and designs. Eventually, they became popular with Mexican art world high-flyers Diego Rivera and Frida Kahlo, who bought and displayed them in their homes.

Nowadays, though, it's the Oaxacan type of *alebrije* that's arguably better known. After catching wind of the Mexico City iterations, local carvers began creating delicate *alebrijes* with copal wood – woodcarving was already a popular regional craft – that were then intricately painted. Common animals depicted include armadillos, cats and dragons, and while Oaxacan *alebrijes* are often said to represent Zapotec *nahuales* (spirit guardians), it's a broadly debunked theory, likely intended to add a dash of spice and "authenticity" to what's actually a recent invention. They may not quite have the mystical heritage many assume, but they remain an irreverent and beloved example of Mexico's contemporary handicrafts.

Mexican Literature

Shamans spinning tales of the cosmos, feminists penning political verse, novelists forging surreal new genres: Mexico's literary canon has been shaped by generations of innovators.

Contemporary Mexican literature has slowly cemented its position on the world stage, with translations read by global audiences and young writers nominated for prestigious awards. But behind Mexico's cutting-edge publishing is a lineage of social challengers who have forged a remarkable, and often distinctly political, literary canon.

THE FIRST STORIES

Oral storytelling in the form of poems, prayers, myths and invocations marked the start of Mexico's literary tradition. For the first great civilizations – the Olmecs, Aztecs and Mayans – story-telling was a primary means of making sense of the cosmos, and origin stories (*p50*) were narrated as a form of collective ritual, often by shamans trained in the art of storytelling. While the Mayans were one of the first societies in Mexico to develop complex glyphs and pictographs, they were oral storytellers, leaving behind little written testimony.

THE WRITTEN WORD

Indigenous storytelling was irrevocably altered by the arrival of the Latin alphabet in the 16th century. A new era of written testimony dawned, with conquistadors like Bernal Díaz del Castillo penning accounts of Mexico's Indigenous peoples, including *The Conquest of New Spain* (1568), which were read by audiences in Europe. Importantly, Indigenous storytellers also made use of the new alphabet, preserving traditional wisdom in written texts. Illustrated works including 16th-century Aztec codices and parts of the Mayan epic *Chilim Balam* were handwritten by scribes through-out the 17th and 18th centuries.

MEXICAN BAROQUE

By the 17th century, the clash of Indigenous wisdom with Catholic theology gave rise to a new movement: the Mexican Baroque. This dense but comic mode, defined by religious or political themes, was initially influenced by Spanish intellectuals in Mexico, with Antonio de Solís y Ribadeneyra's *Historia de la conquista de México* (1684) hailed as a prose classic. The

Above left The nun and Baroque poet Sor Juana Inés de la Cruz

Above right English-language cover of Mariano Azuela's *Los de Abajo* (1920)

Mexican nun Sor Juana Inés de la Cruz (1648–1695) was a pioneering Baroque poet, with proto-feminist works like *Primero sueño* (First Dream, 1692) eloquently defending women's right to an intel-lectual life. Recognized as a pioneer by Catholics in her day, she was fondly referred to as "The Phoenix of America", and her writings paved the way for a new school of political writing.

SPEAKING TRUTH TO POWER

Mexico's Baroque style would dominate the literary scene until the War of Independence, when politically charged writers began to grapple with ideas of national autonomy. In 1816, as the struggle raged on, Mexican writer José Joaquín Fernández de Lizardi wrote

El Periquillo Sarniento (The Mangy Parrot). This trenchant political work is now hailed as the first Latin American novel, written at a pivotal moment in Mexico's history. By following the adventures of the morally dubious character Pedro Sarmiento, the novel exposes the corruption of the Spanish administration; the critique proved popular with the Mexican public, though the last volumes of the book were heavily censored by the government.

The political power of Mexican literature was heightened during the revolution (1910–1917), when young writers like Mariano Azuela published visceral accounts of the country's conflict. His seminal 1920 novel *Los de Abajo* (The Underdogs) detailed the social and political experiences of agricultural labourers during the revolution. Translated into English soon after publication, it was one of Mexico's first international bestsellers, with readers captivated by tales of the revolutionary war.

THE LATIN AMERICAN BOOM

The success of *Los de Abajo* was followed by a huge increase in Mexico's global publishing. In the mid-20th century, the so-called Latin American Boom saw Mexican writers like Carlos Fuentes achieve global circulation, with audiences hungry for Latin America's inventive writing. This was largely due to the birth of magical realism, a genre which blends social realism with fantasy.

Colombian author Gabriel García Márquez's *Cien Años de Soledad* (One Hundred Years of Solitude, 1967) might be seen as the defining example of magical realism, but he was very much inspired by Mexican writer Elena Garro's *Los recuerdos del porvenir* (Recollections of Things to Come, 1969).

Around the same time, pioneering Mexican poets like Nobel Prize-winning Octavio Paz were rethinking the parameters of verse. Paz's politically charged early works questioned the importance of faith, heritage and activism.

NEW VOICES

Politics still fuels the literature of today, with a new generation of impassioned

LIBRO ... AJARA INTERNATIONAL ... F. A IN

#YaMeCansé

No porque
mañana pueda ser
yo,
sino porque hoy

Villoro

Above Carmen Aristegui and Lydia Cacho protesting about threats to writers

Left Octavio Paz, centre left, with students at Cornell University

novelists penning charged works in inventive styles. The last decade has seen a resurgence in interest in the country's literary output, with women writers including Fernanda Melchor and Brenda Navarro leading the charge. A group of fearless investigative journalists, meanwhile, including Carmen Aristegui and Lydia Cacho, are spearheading a wave of incisive non-fiction which targets government corruption, despite threats of intimidation and censorship.

A Latin American literary power, Mexico today has the most successful publishing industry in the region. Storytelling remains an important means of challenging the status quo while grappling with life's stark realities.

SEMINAL WORKS

Pedro Páramo (1955) by Juan Rulfo

A cornerstone of magical realism, *Pedro Páramo* recounts a man's journey to the fictional ghost town of Comala.

Aura (1962) by Carlos Fuentes

Fuentes was a leading figure of the Latin American Boom, and *Aura*, a Gothic novella, is a fine example of magical realism.

Battles in the Desert (1981) by José Emilio Pacheco

A gripping tale set in post-WWII Mexico City, this novel explores a teen's love for his classmate's mother.

A Massacre in Mexico (2018) by Elena Poniatowska

A harrowing account of the 1968 massacre of students in a Tlatelolco square.

ARChitecture aND DesiGN

Encompassing Mesoamerican pyramids, colonial-era churches and contemporary structures, Mexico's architecture charts the evolution of the nation.

Think of Mexico's most famous buildings and the pyramid of Chichén Itzá or the Basilica of Our Lady of Guadalupe might come to mind. Vestiges of past civiliz-ations and the nation's colonial period, these structures are spectacular, but they're just a small part of Mexico's architectural story. With 35 UNESCO World Heritage Sites and numerous modern marvels, the country's structures tell a story of innovation, conquest and national pride.

MESOAMERICAN ARCHITECTURE

Mexico's Mesoamerican empires were among the world's first architectural pioneers. The Mayans and Aztecs produced one of the country's most recognizable architectural forms: the stepped pyramid (p184). Built to mirror the mountains of central and southern Mexico, these soaring, four-sided structures were constructed from heaped earthen mounds that were covered with huge stones; these were arranged in a stepped style known as *talud-tablero*, which helped give pyramids their distinct form and multiple sloping tiers.

Many pyramids were built according to the principles of astronomy, including the Temple of Kukulcán (also known as El Castillo) at Chichén Itzá in Yucatán state. This structure has 365 steps in total, one for each day of the Mayan solar calendar. Pyramids were often topped with temples, too, which were

Plaza of the Three Cultures

The best visual representation of Mexico's primary architectural periods is the Plaza da las Tres Culturas (Plaza of the Three Cultures) in Mexico City. Opened in 1964, the plaza showcases the country's three defining styles: the ruins of the Aztec-built Tlatelolco pyramid complex, the Templo de Santiago Apóstol, built over the pyramid by the Spanish in the 16th century, and the modern tower of the Centro Cultural Universitario.

Above The Baroque Santo Domingo in Oaxaca

themselves crowned with roof combs, decorative elements thought to resemble the headdresses worn by rulers.

SPANISH AESTHETICS

In an attempt to assert dominance over the area, and to evangelize the Indigenous population, the colonizing Spanish built Catholic structures over sacred sites, including temples, often using the very stone from the structures that they had destroyed.

These first structures were often entire monastery complexes rather than single churches, largely because the earliest missionaries were led by Franciscan, Dominican and Augustinian monks. Fortress-like in appearance, they were built with high walls that ensured privacy and prevented attacks. The monasteries also incorporated open space in their designs, including large atriums and open-air chapels. It is thought that this was to encourage the conversion of the Indigenous population, who were used to worshipping outdoors.

Mexico's colonial buildings were largely dictated by European fashions, with the symmetry of Renaissance styles giving way to the bold statements of the Baroque. Many buildings in central Mexico, the first area under Spanish control, are Baroque in style; examples are best seen in Puebla, whose cityscape is sprinkled with vast cupolas and tall bell towers.

STORIES FROM MEXICO

My family has lived for generations in this old area of Mexico City. I founded ReUrbano to rehabilitate many of the historic buildings that unfortunately lay deteriorated and often abandoned.

While studying architecture at the National Autonomous University of Mexico, I had the opportunity to study abroad in Spain, where I discovered how architects in Barcelona had reworked historic buildings for modern use. I knew the same could be done in Mexico City, conserving the tradition and culture of many of its iconic neighbourhoods.

And many younger Mexicans are looking to return to the city centre, eschewing car culture in favour of using public transport, bicycles and walking. Such parking-free residences are still restricted to certain parts of the city, but ReUrbano's projects have helped revitalize neighbourhoods and increase foot traffic. This work gives ReUrbano a unique role in conserving Mexican heritage.

Rodrigo Rivero Borrell, architect and founder of ReUrbano, Mexico City

EUROPEAN INFLUENCES

European designs continued to dominate following Mexican Independence in 1821 *(p39)*. When Porfirio Díaz became president in 1876, he instigated a period of modernization, largely by imitating the aesthetics of a now-industrialized Europe.

A focus was placed upon public buildings, which were designed by foreign architects. Mexico City's Palacio Postal, for instance, was built by Italian architect Adamo Boari and incorporated elements of Spanish Rococo, Art Nouveau and Spanish Renaissance Revival. Small nods to Mexico's Indigenous past were incorporated into some building projects; statues of Aztec rulers Cuauhtémoc and Cuitláhuac were added to the Paseo de la Reforma, alongside depictions of jaguars and other animals important in Mesoamerican cosmology. Yet these additions were minor, and Mexican architecture continued to look to Europe.

PRACTICAL DESIGNS

During the 20th century, massive migrations of people from rural areas into cities *(p26)* shifted the government's focus towards the construction of schools, hospitals and housing.

This period of Modernist urban building brought architects like José Villagran García, Juan O'Gorman and Luis Barragán to the fore. They found inspiration in the ideas of Swiss-French architect Le Corbusier and the Bauhaus movement, and most importantly in Functionalism – the principle that buildings should be designed for a specific purpose, with practical materials and little ornament. The style captured the ethos of a post-Independence Mexico on a mission to modernize. Among the projects

Above left The Pedro Vélez centre, designed by Rozana Montiel in 2022

Above right Luis Barragán's Casa Gilardi (1975) in Mexico City

erected during this time was the massive campus of the National Autonomous University of Mexico, which was constructed using brick, glass and reinforced concrete.

CONTEMPORARY CREATIONS
Mexican architecture continues to be influenced by global trends. That's not to say the country's architects lack innovation, however. Some have taken progressive approaches, spearheading socially focused and sustainable projects.

Among them is Mauricio Rocha, who created the Center for the Blind and Visually Impaired in Mexico City, which incorporated sound-insulated booths. Rozana Montiel designed the striking Pedro Vélez community centre in the capital, with open walkways and a multipurpose central courtyard redolent of the spacious atriums used in monasteries and temples of old. Harking back to old designs while looking ahead to a sustainable future, these architects are carving out Mexico's modern styles.

Statement Structures

Mexican architecture is a synthesis of eras, regional influences and international styles. From the glory of Indigenous empires, through 300 years of colonial rule to today's global nation, Mexico's structures are monuments to the forces that have shaped the country. Here are a few of the defining architectural structures from the past 3,000 years.

PYRAMIDS

Few buildings represent ancient Mexico better than the stepped pyramids constructed by Mesoamerican civilizations, such as the Olmec and Mayans. The three most famous pyramids are those dedicated to the Sun and Moon in the ancient city of Teotihuacán, and El Castillo (The Castle) in Chichén Itzá. The Pyramid of the Sun is the largest building in the city of Teotihuacán, and one of the tallest constructed by the Mesoamerican empires. Though the pyramid's function is shrouded in mystery, it's believed that a temple once crowned the structure.

MISSIONS

Mexico's mission architecture developed as Spanish missionaries pushed north from Mexico City into the northern grasslands. Missions were established as defensive settlements to protect the European arrivals from often-hostile locals, and were built from adobe and stone. Both the residential settlements and the churches at the mission's centre featured thick walls, small windows, arched doors and breezeways to offset the heat.

CATHEDRALS

Mexico's array of stunning cathedrals showcases the influence of European styles, and their size and grandeur was a key means of asserting Catholic dominance. The imposing Catedral Metropolitana, in Mexico City, is Latin America's largest cathedral. It blends Baroque and Neo-Classical styles, and it's rumoured that conquistador Hernán Cortés laid the first stone as his forces travelled north.

ADOBE

Though adobe is often considered an architectural style in itself, it's technically a building material: adobe bricks are made from mud formed largely of straw and clay. By the end of the colonial period, adobe was the main material for the building of rural churches and basic housing due to its cheapness and abundance. It has since fallen out of use, partly due to concerns around hygiene and to the popularity of newer and cheaper materials like cement.

MODERN DESIGNS

Since the mid-20th century, Mexico's urban construction has been dominated by architectural trends from outside the country. Mexican architects and designers nod towards the country's past, however, with exterior decorations, often in the form of murals. The Central Library of the National Autonomous University of Mexico is decorated with a vast mural by Juan O'Gorman representing the country's diverse demographics.

1 The vast pyramid of Teotihuacán

2 Misión de Nuestra Señora de Loreto Conchó, a mission-style church in Loreto, Baja California Sur

3 Catedral Metropolitana in Mexico City

4 Traditional adobe constructions at the ruins of Paquimé, in Chihuahua

5 Mexican painter Juan O'Gorman's mural on the National Autonomous University's Central Library

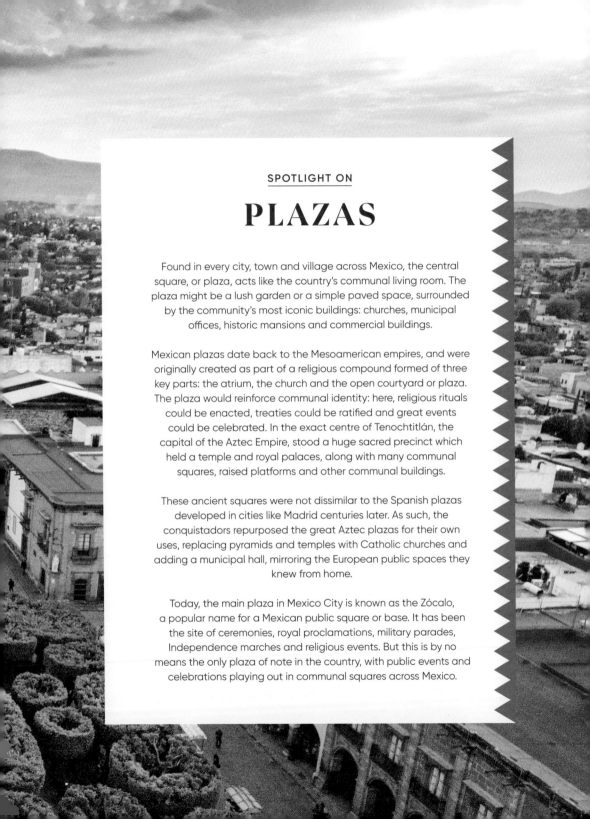

PLAZAS

Found in every city, town and village across Mexico, the central square, or plaza, acts like the country's communal living room. The plaza might be a lush garden or a simple paved space, surrounded by the community's most iconic buildings: churches, municipal offices, historic mansions and commercial buildings.

Mexican plazas date back to the Mesoamerican empires, and were originally created as part of a religious compound formed of three key parts: the atrium, the church and the open courtyard or plaza. The plaza would reinforce communal identity: here, religious rituals could be enacted, treaties could be ratified and great events could be celebrated. In the exact centre of Tenochtitlán, the capital of the Aztec Empire, stood a huge sacred precinct which held a temple and royal palaces, along with many communal squares, raised platforms and other communal buildings.

These ancient squares were not dissimilar to the Spanish plazas developed in cities like Madrid centuries later. As such, the conquistadors repurposed the great Aztec plazas for their own uses, replacing pyramids and temples with Catholic churches and adding a municipal hall, mirroring the European public spaces they knew from home.

Today, the main plaza in Mexico City is known as the Zócalo, a popular name for a Mexican public square or base. It has been the site of ceremonies, royal proclamations, military parades, Independence marches and religious events. But this is by no means the only plaza of note in the country, with public events and celebrations playing out in communal squares across Mexico.

Celebrating Mexico

Given Mexico's sizeable Catholic population, it's no surprise that countless Catholic festivals help mark the progress of the year. Christmas, Easter and the Día de la Virgen de Guadalupe are major highlights of the country's cultural calendar, each being celebrated with both pomp and circumstance and by much more intimate family gatherings. Such religious celebrations are often blended with Indigenous festivities, creating events where heavenly saints are honoured in the same breath as ancient gods. Beyond religious festivities, though, Mexicans can always find a reason to celebrate, whether they're toasting big life moments, honouring national pride or ringing in the New Year.

HONOURING DEATH

Known around the world for its vibrant, eye-catching costumes and colourful face paint, Día de los Muertos (Day of the Dead) is one of the most important celebrations in Mexico.

According to Mexican tradition, every year the dead have divine permission to visit their friends and relatives on earth. The gates of heaven are said to open on 1 November, allowing the spirits of children to return to the world of the living and rejoin their families for 24 hours; on 2 November, the same is believed to happen for the souls of adults. Yet far from being a time of sadness, this vibrant yet intimate occasion is seen as an opportunity to remember, honour and reconnect with lost loved ones.

ORIGINS OF DÍA DE LOS MUERTOS

The beginnings of the Day of the Dead stretch back to the Mesoamerican cultures, including the Aztecs and Toltecs, if not before then. For these groups, death was seen as a natural and ever-present part of life, and something that was to be celebrated rather than mourned. They believed that the departed travelled to Chicunamictlán, the Land of the Dead; this realm was made up of nine levels that the dead then travelled through to reach Mictlán, their final resting place. In order to help them

on their journey (thought to take several years), family members would leave offerings of food, water and tools on graves and altars. This act was performed just after they'd passed, and then again every August during a month-long celebration; the event was tied to paying tribute to Mictecacihuatl and

Goddess of Death

The Aztecs recognized many different gods, among them Mictecacihuatl, the goddess of death and the underworld. According to legend, she was sacrificed as a baby before becoming ruler of the underworld, where she married Mictlantecuhtli. Often depicted as having the face of a skull, with a gaping, grinning jaw, she was believed to protect the bones of the dead, which, according to the Aztecs, could then be used by other gods to create new life.

Mictlantecuhtli, the married goddess and god who together were believed to rule the underworld.

The Spanish arrived in Mexico in the 16th century, bringing their Catholic traditions with them, including All Souls' Day, which was celebrated on 2 November. On this day, Catholics pray for the souls of baptized individuals who have died and yet are stuck in purgatory due to their sins; it is believed that by praying they may help to cleanse the souls of the dead and allow them to reach heaven. Such ideas of helping the departed on their way provided a link between the two events and, over time, they merged to become Día de los Muertos.

MODERN-DAY CELEBRATIONS

Similar to the Aztecs hundreds of years ago, today family members create colourful *ofrendas*, or altars, at home. These are a way to help guide departed spirits back from Chicunamictlán. Gently illuminated by glowing candles, these shrines are usually decorated with crosses, images of ancestors and a variety of offerings. Among them are brightly coloured *calaveras de azúcar* (sugar skulls), whose sweetness is said to counteract the darkness of death, and *cempasúchil*, a type of marigold flower native to Mexico; their glow is believed to offer a beacon guiding loved ones on their journey. More personal items are

included, too, such as the favourite food or trinket of a loved one; for any children, a much-loved toy may be added.

Each *ofrenda* must also include items that correspond to the four elements: water, earth, air and fire. For the first, a glass of water is set upon the altar, so departed souls can quench their thirst after their journey back from the after-life. Favourite family dishes are often used to represent earth and provide nourishment to the dead, while *papel picado* (tissue paper that's been cut into elaborate designs) signifies both air and, when stirred by the breeze, the return of once-lost loved ones. Then, of course, there are the candles, which stand in for fire and help to guide departed spirits back home. Copal, a type of resinous incense, is often burnt, as a way to cleanse the space of negative energy and help the spirits of the dead to return.

Outside of the home, plazas and other public spaces will often be draped in more *papel picado*. The paper, as it catches the wind, serves as a gentle reminder of life's fragility. Papier-mâché skeletons are also displayed publicly, often in comical poses or engaged in everyday activities – such a willingness to laugh and find joy in the presence of death is key to the celebration.

Many Mexicans will visit the graves of loved ones in a cemetery. During the day, these places of rest are cleaned and offerings, similar to those placed on the *ofrendas*, are left. Such acts mirror those which were once taken during

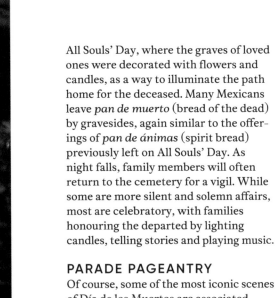

All Souls' Day, where the graves of loved ones were decorated with flowers and candles, as a way to illuminate the path home for the deceased. Many Mexicans leave *pan de muerto* (bread of the dead) by gravesides, again similar to the offerings of *pan de ánimas* (spirit bread) previously left on All Souls' Day. As night falls, family members will often return to the cemetery for a vigil. While some are more silent and solemn affairs, most are celebratory, with families honouring the departed by lighting candles, telling stories and playing music.

PARADE PAGEANTRY

Of course, some of the most iconic scenes of Día de los Muertos are associated with the event's colourful parades and dances, complete with costumed participants. These take place across Mexico, whether it's the lively carnival-style processions that wind through some neighbourhoods in Oaxaca or the throngs of Indigenous women wearing bright, embroidered dresses who dance through the streets of San Cristobal de las Casas. These events are a reminder to the living that death is an integral part of life and those who dance today will one day be among the dead, so they should enjoy life as much as possible while they can.

Skulls and skeletons are a major part of Día de los Muertos, too. These symbols are long-standing elements of the celebrations – the Aztecs used skulls in their ceremonies – and continue to be a regular feature, including in San Agustín Etla's eye-catching La Muerteada. Here, locals don skull masks, among other kinds, and roam the city's streets until dawn; they also wear mirrors, thought to scare witches away, and ring bells to guide spirits home to earth.

DAY OF THE DEAD FOODS

Sugar skulls

Made at home or bought from a local market stall, these bright, crystalline skulls are a ubiquitous feature of the festival. Sugar art was brought to Mexico by 17th-century Italian missionaries and quickly became an important method of crafting religious icons, largely because sugar was cheaper and more abundant than stone. While most of these skulls are merely decorative, smaller, edible options are also made as a snack.

Pan de muerto

This "bread of the dead" is a traditional sweet pastry that originated in Aztec societies of centuries past. It is placed on the altar as an offering and also enjoyed as a treat during the festival. Round in shape, with a pair of crossed bones and a circle representing a skull on top, the *pan de muerto* is similar in texture to Jewish challah bread, and is usually sprinkled with sugar or other toppings.

Calabaza en tacha

This candied pumpkin is commonly found on *ofrendas* during Día de los Muertos. It is prepared by simmering chunks of pumpkin in water alongside Piloncillo (a type of unrefined cane sugar) and spices like cinnamon, cloves or star anise.

STORIES FROM MEXICO

In the city of Oaxaca, where I grew up, Día de los Muertos was one of the most important holidays of the year. I remember celebrating it with my family when I was a child. For kids, there was such a feeling of joy and excitement in the air as November approached.

Preparations began in mid-October, when ingredients for dishes like mole and tamales were purchased. As the celebration got closer, we'd also buy other important items for the *ofrenda*, including fruit, flowers and candles, plus things that the deceased used to enjoy, such as chocolate and mezcal. We'd also bake *pan de muerto*, made out of eggs and butter, and decorated with sesame seeds and sugar.

The whole family participated in setting up the *ofrenda* and at some point everyone would gather before the altar to pray. As children, we were warned not to eat anything from the altar before the arrival of the dead, otherwise they could become angry. But afterwards, we'd devour the sugar skulls labeled with our names. It was always such a fun holiday, and one deeply rooted in tradition.

Pedro Velásquez Martínez,
Oaxaca City

One of the most well-known sights of Día de los Muertos are the *calaveras*. Inspired by José Guadalupe Posada's cartoon figure La Catrina (*p198*), many female parade participants have taken to dressing in the same style as this laughing skeleton, donning long, flowing dresses and painting their faces to imitate skulls.

THE GLOBAL FESTIVAL

The vibrant aesthetic and varied symbols of the festival – especially La Catrina – are no longer confined to Mexico, and the celebration is recognized around the world. Many US cities with sizable Mexican populations, including Los Angeles, Chicago and San Antonio, hold large celebrations and parades. Los Angeles' Hollywood Forever Cemetery hosts the largest Día de los Muertos celebration outside of Mexico, replete with processions, decorated banners and a kaleidoscope of vivid costumes.

The festival is entrenched in global popular culture, too, with a plethora of films and TV shows making the most of its unique colour palette. The 2015 James Bond film *Spectre* featured a fictional Day of the Dead parade in Mexico City. Such was the popularity of the scene that the city's government decided that life should imitate art, and opted to host its first parade in 2016. Social media has also played a role in the global popularity

Above A Día de los Muertos parade in Oaxaca

of Día de los Muertos, spurred on by the event's eye-catching imagery, such as multicoloured *papel picado* and striking skull face paint.

This global popularity is not without its complications. Some fear that the festival has been commodified and divested of its spiritual associations, with revellers – including visitors to Mexico – latching onto the performance but disregarding its traditional values. Mexicans are keen to ensure that those participating in Día de los Muertos recognize its roots and strive to maintain its integrity, including by reiterating the difference between the festival and more commodified Halloween celebrations. For many around the world, however, the festival represents a vital opportunity to approach death from a new angle. It brings the darkest of subjects into the open, dismantling death's taboos and bringing families together in joyous remembrance of those loved and lost.

ON THE MAP

DAY OF THE DEAD

Mexico's Día de los Muertos celebrations are wonderfully rich and varied, with different regions often marking the event in unique ways, whether through Indigenous folk dances, skeleton-filled parades or candlelit graveside vigils. However it's celebrated, the Day of the Dead is always a heartfelt tribute to loved ones, embracing death as an inseparable part of life. This map showcases some of the ways that Mexicans honour this most important of events.

Aguascalientes' capital hosts the Festival de las Calaveras (Festival of Skulls), an event dedicated to La Catrina *(p198)*; her creator, the artist José Guadalupe Posada, was born here. During the event, the city centre becomes the scene of the Parade of Skulls, complete with skeleton costumes, themed floats and live music.

In **Michoacán** on the night of 1 November, families row boats festooned with candles and flowers to the island of Janitzio on Lake Patzcuaro. They then undertake a candlelit procession to the cemetery, where they gather to chant, sing and spend the night among the spirits of their loved ones.

In the capital of **Oaxaca**, the streets are adorned with tapestries made with coloured sand, sawdust and flower petals. These intricate designs feature depictions of saints, geometric patterns or skeletons. The decorations only last a day or two – a fitting symbol of the ephemeral nature of life.

Referred to as Xantolo in the **Huasteca** region,
Día de los Muertos is celebrated with folk dances
called *cuadrillas*. Here, the interaction between
life and death is played out with a diverse cast of
characters including a charro (cowboy), elderly
people, a pregnant woman, the devil and Death.

Around Mérida in the state of
Yucatán, Día de los Muertos is known
as Hanal Pixan or "food of the gods".
A special feast is prepared for the
spirits, featuring a unique dish reserved
for the occasion: *mucbipollo*, a large
tamale made with chicken and pork,
wrapped in banana leaves and
cooked in an underground pit.

The town of Chignahuapan in **Puebla**
hosts the Festival de la Luz y la Vida
(Festival of Light and Life), an event that
originated in an Aztec purification ritual.
Carrying torches, dancers parade from
the town square to an illuminated floating
pyramid in a lagoon, where they perform
a lively dance representing the journey
of the souls through the underworld.

La CATRINA

One of the most iconic images of Mexico's Día de los Muertos celebrations is La Calavera Catrina, popularly known as La Catrina, a female skeleton swathed in an ostentatious turn-of-the-century dress. Like much of Mexico's Day of the Dead festivities, this character may have her roots in ancient Aztec culture, which venerated Mictecacihuatl, the goddess of death *(p190)*. La Catrina as an image in popular culture, however, emerged centuries later, thanks to an etching by the cartoon artist José Guadalupe Posada.

In the early 20th century, Posada created a character originally known as "La Calavera Garbancera", intended to mock new moneyed Mexicans who rejected their own Indigenous traditions in favour of the latest European customs and fashions: the laughing skeleton is rendered somewhat preposterous by Posada's etching with her frilly hat and fancy dress. "Death is democratic," wrote Posada, "because at the end of the day, fair or dark-skinned, rich or poor, everyone ends up a skeleton."

The sentiment struck a chord with Mexicans – unsurprising in a country known for its often darkly humorous approach to death *(p142)*. Over the following years, La Catrina became entrenched in Mexican culture, with artists like Diego Rivera *(p164)* including her in their works. Today, this eye-catching skeleton has become a favourite costume choice for Día de los Muertos parade participants, helping to spread her fame all around the world.

Catholic Celebrations

Día de los Muertos might be Mexico's biggest religious festival, but there are also plenty of Catholic celebrations shaping the country's calendar, from Christmas to Easter and beyond.

With around four-fifths of the population followers of the faith, it's no surprise that Catholic celebrations are important in Mexico. These religious festivities bring communities together to celebrate and demonstrate their devotion to God and the saints – especially the Virgin of Guadalupe, Mexico's beloved patron saint.

FESTIVE HAPPENINGS

As in so many places around the world, as the year comes to an end Mexicans get ready to celebrate Christmas. In line with Catholic traditions, a variety of events are held over four festive weeks.

Things kick off in mid-December with a series of *posadas*. Taking place over nine consecutive nights, each *posada* begins with a procession – a re-enactment of Mary and Joseph's search for shelter (*posadas* is the Spanish word for "inns") – followed by group carol singing outside a chosen house, and then a party. As society has become increasingly secular, new *posada* trends have emerged, with piñatas, often in the shape of a seven-point star, becoming a staple – one beloved by children. In some Mexican cities, the festive spirit continues well into the night, with carol singing giving way to large gatherings. For many, *posadas* are an important part of the Christmas festivities, for their role in celebrating the story of Jesus's birth and bringing communities together.

The final *posada* is held on Noche Buena (Christmas Eve), with families then going on to church for the Misa de Gallo (mass of the rooster), followed by a celebratory family meal and the exchanging of presents. After so many days of festivities, Christmas Day itself is more relaxed, with families spending quality time together.

But celebrations aren't over after 25 December. In fact, the festive season lasts until El Día de Los Reyes Magos, or Three Kings Day on 6 January. The day honours the three wise men who visited the manger after the birth of Jesus, and is marked by the traditional cutting and eating of the *rosca de reyes*. This sweet, ring-shaped bread is often decorated with colourful candy or fruit and contains within it a hidden surprise: a tiny plastic baby Jesus. Whoever finds Jesus in their slice of bread gets to host a party on El Día de la Candelaria on 2 February, an intimate event marking the presentation of Jesus in the temple of Jerusalem.

Above Children taking part in a festive procession

Right Parade celebrating Three Kings Day

EASTER EVENTS

Unsurprisingly, Easter is another big event in Mexico's Catholic calendar. It begins with Semana Santa, or Holy Week, honouring Jesus's final days before the crucifixion. Taking place around March or April, the celebration typically lasts two weeks, starting on Palm Sunday and ending on Easter Sunday. Many cities with large Catholic populations, such as Taxco and Oaxaca, put on vibrant festivals, which include lively re-enactments of the Passion of the Christ. Processions also take place in Mexico City, with those in the district of Iztapalapa famously elaborate: an actor is often elected to play Jesus and huge crowds turn out to watch as the drama unfolds.

Easter Sunday sees further processions, with effigies of Christ and the Virgin Mary. Many families will attend a sombre mass early in the day, which is followed by more light-hearted festivities, with fireworks displays, dancing and orchestras filling the cities. A more unusual sight is the practice of self-flagellation, particularly associated with the city of Taxco. Both men and women can be seen lugging hay bales or large crosses on their backs for long distances, and some even whip themselves with thorny branches.

CELEBRATING SAINTS

Many of Mexico's celebrations revolve around individual Catholic saints. One of the most revered is Santiago Apostol (St James the Apostle), the patron saint of Spain. Many towns and villages are named for him and his feast day, 25 July, is celebrated throughout the country with the Dance of the Tastoanes, a re-enactment of Mesoamerican peoples fighting Spanish conquistadors.

Across Mexico, different towns and regions have adopted different saints, sometimes according to the needs of their communities. In downtown Mexico City, for instance, many poorer residents revere San Judas (St Jude), who is said to help with money problems. Each month, at the Hipolito church in downtown Mexico City, crowds gather for masses dedicated to the saint.

Mexico's biggest religious festival dedicated to a religious figure takes

Above A parade in
Guanajuato marking
Semana Santa

Left A Good Friday
procession in
Guanajuato state

place on 12 December. On this day,
pilgrims from all over the country make
their way to Mexico City to honour the
Virgin of Guadalupe at the holy basilica
dedicated in her name (*p68*). Pre-dawn
mass services start off the day, before
attendees enjoy float-filled parades and
traditional Aztec dance performances
(the ground on which the basilica complex stands was sacred to Indigenous
peoples). Altars overflowing with
flowers and candles for the Virgin line
the city's streets, mariachi bands play
throughout the day and fireworks
crackle through the night. It's a day
that unites people through faith, family
and fun, with the Virgin of Guadalupe
a beloved symbol of protection throughout the country.

Narco Saints

Dressed in a white robe and often
wielding a scythe and a globe, Santa
Muerte – a mix of the Grim Reaper
and the Virgin of Guadalupe – is just
one of a rapidly growing number of
"narco saints". Another is Jesús
Malverde, who is idolized by the poor
communities in the state of Sinaloa,
known for its cartel activity. They are
often worshipped by criminals who
pray to them for protection, riches
and the silence necessary
to mask their dealings.

ON THE MAP

INDIGENOUS CELEBRATIONS

Deeply rooted in Mesoamerican customs and beliefs, Indigenous celebrations are a vibrant blend of spirituality and community. Many originated as ancient customs around the agricultural cycle, but changed over time as a result of the syncretism between Catholicism and the local customs of each Indigenous community.

Easter sees the Rarámuri in **Chihuahua** split into two groups for dances that symbolize the battle between good and evil. Here, the devil's allies wear white body paint, while the defenders of God don traditional clothing and feather headdresses. The event ends with thanks given for the start of a new agricultural cycle.

To ensure a good rainfall and harvest, the Nahua people of Zitlala, **Guerrero**, dress up as jaguars and engage in ritual fights on 5 May. The battles are fierce, with opponents aiming to draw blood – according to tradition, for every drop shed, a drop of rain will fall. But despite the ferocity, there's no animosity between the fighters, who see the engagements as for the good of the community. The event became known as the "tiger fights" after the arrival of the Spanish, who mistook the country's jaguars for tigers.

On the feast day of St Michael (27 September), the Otomi Chichimeca of Tolimán in **Querétaro** give thanks for the previous year's blessings with a *chimal*. This monumental 20-m (66-ft) offering is made with reeds, covered in sotol leaves, and then decorated with flowers, fruit, tortillas, bread and colourful paper. It's then blessed with copal incense, bathed in agave spirits and raised in front of the church, where it will stand until the next year.

During January in Chiapa de Corzo, **Chiapas**, a costumed parade marks the feast days of St Anthony Abbot, St Sebastian and Our Lord of Esquipulas. Donning hand-carved wooden masks, headdresses and colourful serapes, dancers known as *Parachicos* wind through town shaking rattles; the event is considered a collective offering to the saints in anticipation of the coming agricultural cycle.

In July, a huge celebration of Indigenous culture takes place in **Oaxaca**: Guelaguetza. Originally a festival honouring Centeōtl, the maize goddess, the event became a way to pay homage to the Virgin of Carmel during the 18th century. Today, Indigenous communities from across the state perform folk dances in traditional dress. Many dancers throw gifts of chocolate and fruit to the crowd – a reminder that Guelaguetza means "to gift" in the Zapotec language.

COYOLILLO CARNIVAL

Every February, Coyolillo in Veracruz hosts an exuberant carnival honouring the Black heritage of its community. Around 150 years ago, this small town was established by liberated Africans, who had escaped or been freed from enslavement on one of the region's sugar plantations. The community later integrated with local Indigenous groups, yet maintained many of its own unique traditions and beliefs, including this colourful carnival.

Over time, the tradition transformed into the colourful six-day celebration that is enjoyed to this day, involving music, dancing and parades. Food is a big part of the event, with masses of stuffed *chiles rellenos* (stuffed chillies), tamales and pumpkin cakes prepared in advance and lovingly shared with guests and neighbours.

Another crucial element are the wooden masks made especially for the carnival. Carved by hand and painted in colourful hues, these disguises often depict horned animals such as bulls, deer or goats (some with real animal horns attached), and are worn alongside flowered headdresses and vibrant, flowing capes. Many believe that this mask-wearing tradition, which has been passed down through the generations, harks back to the Gule Wamkulu of Mozambique, Malawi and Zambia in West Africa, where men would don similar masks for a ritual dance. Mask-wearing in Coyolillo was once similarly reserved for men; today it's open to women and children, with all taking part in this joyful spectacle.

Family Celebrations

Family gatherings have long been an essential part of Mexican society, strengthening bonds between generations and bringing distant relatives together in mutual celebration.

At the heart of the Mexican social calendar are family get-togethers, joyful events that often tie into religious beliefs. Here, often lavish celebrations accompany rites of passage – baptisms, birthdays and Christmas – and many feature grand ceremonies. These celebrations are adapting to a rapidly globalizing world, with families connecting over longer distances and events changing to reflect the diversity of the country's population.

CATHOLIC GATHERINGS

For Mexico's Catholics, family celebrations are typically grand events, and they begin at the very start of life, with a baptism. Baptisms include a religious ceremony during which the child is washed as a sign of purification, before the parents officially confirm *padrinos* (godparents). Once confirmed, these *padrinos* – usually close and long-standing family friends – play an important role in the baptismal celebration, as they will throughout the child's life. As part of this, they are expected to provide the baptismal gown and to organize a *bolo*, a ritual during which cash is thrown in the air above attending children to symbolize a life of abundance.

Baptisms, like most Catholic celebrations in Mexico, typically involve a substantial guest list, with extended family, close friends and, in rural communities, local neighbours in attendance. After church comes a fiesta that rolls on well into the evening.

Other important Catholic rites celebrated with family include a child's presentation to the church at age three, their first Communion when they approach adolescence and finally the child's confirmation.

GETTING MARRIED

Perhaps the most lavish of all the Catholic rites, weddings in Mexico are often spectacularly lengthy affairs and can be defined by an array of rituals. The act of the *lazo*, for instance, sees a large rosary looped over the *novios*, or bride and groom, to signify their union during the nuptials. There's also the old custom of the *baile del billete* ("money dance"), which involves guests pinning money to the bride and groom's clothes (traditionally a plain suit for the groom and a simple white

Above An Oaxacan wedding with a *mono de calenda* of the bride to the right

dress for the bride, with Spanish-influenced touches including the light bolero jacket and the flowing mantilla veil).

Though traditional Catholic weddings remain popular, these celebrations vary significantly across the country. In Veracruz, it's typical to tuck into *zacahuil* (a large tamale), while Oaxaca sees wedding parties dance down the streets in post-ceremony *calendas* (parades), alongside huge *monos de calenda* (oversized papier-mâché models of the bride and groom). Indigenous communities with Mayan heritage, meanwhile,

might opt for a Mayan ceremony officiated by a spiritual priest or shaman. These ceremonies typically feature aromatic clouds of copal incense, with the bride adorned in a simple white *huipil* dress and the groom in a plain, white suit.

Marriage ceremonies are adapting to reflect modern Mexican culture, too. In June 2023, thousands of couples celebrated the countrywide legalization of same-sex civil marriage with a mass civil ceremony in Mexico City. Hundreds of joint weddings were officiated amid fluttering rainbow banners, a joyous celebration of love and equality.

STORIES FROM MEXICO

I've seen so many celebrations of baptism and Communion in my life from both family and friends and I remember going through my own sacraments. My family was very strict about our faith and we went to church every Sunday and my mother always had a biblical story to weave into everyday moments. I loved being involved in my cousins' baptisms as I got older and the parties we'd have after. It shaped how I felt families should help each other and my values of what it means to be Catholic.

What I remember most about my own confirmation ceremony was how much stress I felt to prove that I would be a devout person for the rest of my life. It felt like such a big responsibility and I was only 16 years old, I wasn't sure how to step into this adult role. But once the ceremony was over, I felt better coming home in my white dress to my family, who were ready to celebrate and seemed so happy for me. That's the takeaway for me: the sense of having family support in hard and happy times.

Mariana Garcia,
Massachusetts, US

RITES OF PASSAGE

Yet family gatherings aren't confined to baptisms and weddings. Birthdays are blowout affairs, soundtracked by Mexico's very own birthday song, "Las mañanitas" ("Little Mornings"), popularized by the mariachi bands who are often invited to perform at milestone birthdays. Mexican birthday parties typically feature all the familiar trappings – gifts, snacks, drinks and cake – with a particularly playful twist. After blowing out the birthday candles, the rhythmic *"mor-di-da, mor-di-da"* ("bite it") chant begins in earnest. As soon as the birthday boy or girl leans in for a bite, a devious relative swoops in to push their face into the cake.

Without a doubt, the biggest birthday
event in any Mexican family is the
quinceaños. Traditionally a religious
milestone marking a girl's 15th birthday
and entry into womanhood, this event
has turned into a blowout party. It's
common to get dressed up for a pre-
party photoshoot, during which
quinceañeras bustle around town in
puffy, sparkly ball gowns, complete
with coiffed hair and a tiara. While some
traditions are seen as overly traditional
and outdated – including gifting high

heels to mark the *quinceañera*'s newfound womanhood – others remain
ubiquitous, such as selecting a group
of *damas* (maids, typically female
friends) and *chambelanes* (chamber-
lains, usually young male friends) to
perform a choreographed dance at the
party. While these celebrations have
traditionally been for girls only, the
21st century has seen the advent of
similar celebrations for boys of the
same age – giving Mexican families
yet another reason to celebrate.

National Pride

In a country where public radio broadcasts the national anthem twice daily, civic pride is a big deal. National celebrations are a way to celebrate the country and its history, and are often grand affairs.

Mexicans rarely pass up an excuse to celebrate, and the country observes several dates during the year to remember key historical and cultural events. There are 12 official *días festivos* (public holidays), some of which honour important anniversaries with grand ceremonies.

MARKING INDEPENDENCE

Perhaps the greatest national event of all is Independence Day, a celebration rooted in the legendary events of 16 September 1810. On this day, in the city of Dolores Hidalgo in Guanajuato, insurgent priest Father Miguel Hidalgo issued a rallying call now known as the "Cry of Dolores". He rang his church bell, so the story goes, and urged the nation to cast off the shackles of Spanish colonial rule. Mexico's War of Independence was so launched, though it would be 11 long years until liberation from Spain was achieved.

For many, this event is a highlight of the cultural calendar: a time to celebrate the birth of the modern nation and take pride in what it means to be Mexican. Tricolour bunting is unfurled, and *chiles en nogada*, with its patriotic colour palette (*p86*), pops up on menus across the country. The whole of September is known as *mes de la patria* (Month of the Fatherland), but the most important event happens on the 15th, when the president takes to the balcony of Mexico City's Palacio Nacional at 11pm to broadcast a re-enactment of Hidalgo's words. "*¡Viva México! ¡Viva México! ¡Viva México!*", goes the cry, echoed by the joyful crowd gathered in the square below.

REVOLUTIONARY PARADES

Although not celebrated with as much fevour, Día de la Revolución (Revolution Day) on 20 November provides another opportunity for Mexicans to honour the country's heritage. This national holiday marks the beginnings of the Mexican Revolution (*p40*), with parades taking place across the country, often featuring children dressed up as revolutionary figures. The biggest procession occurs in Mexico City, where a civic-military parade winds from Zócalo (*p187*) to the Campo Marte, watched by proud locals. A relay race follows, an event that dates to the 1930s and marks the "pacifist and conciliatory will of the people".

CHANGING CELEBRATIONS

While these events draw big crowds, the same isn't true of Día de la Bandera (Flag Day). Held annually on 24 February to

Above A flag-raising ceremony at a primary school in Oaxaca

mark the end of the Mexican War of Independence, it exalts the Mexican flag *(p20)* and the national pride wrapped up in its symbolism. The event is honoured countrywide, with flags raised during military and civic ceremonies, as well as at businesses and schools. A more muted affair it may be, but that's partly down to practicality: as it's not a national holiday, many Mexicans are busy at work. As such, the event is often more readily observed only by the older and more conventionally patriotic generations.

Día de la Constitución (Constitution Day, 5 February) is also more relaxed. While military and civic events do take place on this national holiday – created to mark the signing of Mexico's new constitution in 1917 – an increasing number of Mexicans celebrate in less formal ways, whether with casual picnics or by simply enjoying the long weekend.

Cinco de Mayo

Each year, Pueblans mark the 1862 Battle of Puebla, when French invaders were ousted by the Mexican army, the only war Mexico has conclusively won. Yet while the event is not celebrated in the rest of Mexico, it is in the US. Introduced more widely in the 1960s, Cinco de Mayo became popular among Chicano communities. Nowadays, thanks largely to advertising by beer and tequila companies, the day has become a party north of the border. Detached from its traditional meaning, it's associated with margaritas, sombreros and fiestas.

MODERN FESTIVALS

Whether it's Independence Day or Day of the Dead, many of Mexico's festivals are rooted in heritage. But not all: there's a host of modern celebrations, too, with events focusing on music, LGBTQ+ rights and more.

Set up by enterprising Mexicans, some of the country's modern festivals focus on celebrating local creative talent, while others provide traditionally marginalized communities with ways to make their voices heard – and some do both.

CULTURAL CELEBRATIONS

Mexico's modern music festivals attract global audiences, with a number of large events held annually, and smaller

gatherings catering to listeners of all genres. There's the long-standing Vive Latino in Mexico City, founded in 1998 following a boom in *rock en español* (Spanish rock). Today, the festival still hosts an array of Ibero-American rock acts, but has expanded to other genres, including reggae, and international, English-speaking acts. In the early 2020s, smaller festivals dedicated to on-the-rise *música regional* (regional Mexican music) began to pop up, bringing the focus back to Mexican talent. Chief among these is Arre Fest, set up in 2023.

Aside from music, some of Mexico's most lauded modern events are celebrations of cinema – unsurprising given the country's talent for producing award-winning films and film-makers *(p132)*. The biggest event is June's week-long Guadalajara International Film Festival. Set up in 1986 in an effort to reinvigorate Mexico's waning film industry by promoting Mexican talent, today it's Latin America's largest and most important film-focused event, attracting local and international acting talent and providing screenings of hundreds of films. There's plenty of glitz and glamour, but the main focus continues to be supporting budding

film-makers through programmes such as Talents Guadalajara, which sees the next generation discuss new ideas and approaches with their peers.

SOCIETAL CHANGE-MAKERS

But impactful expression isn't limited to artistic festivals. Some modern events are about campaigning for a fairer, more inclusive future, especially for tradition-ally marginalized sections of society. Mexico City's International Women's Day march, which takes place during March, is one such event; here, women take to the streets of the capital to call for greater rights for women and an end to gender-based violence. The event has helped create wider societal change, with abortion in Mexico City officially

decriminalized in 2007, followed by the rest of the country in 2023.

The LGBTQ+ community, meanwhile, hosts a yearly Pride Parade. This event is an offshoot of the first, more protest-driven march that took place in 1978, during a time when homosexuality was criminalized and stigmatized in Mexico. While the main message of campaigning for greater rights and freedoms continues, the event – which is Latin America's second-largest Pride parade – now has a much more celebratory focus, demon-strating how far LGBTQ+ acceptance has progressed here, especially in Mexico City. And while LGBTQ+ Mexicans still face discrimination, change has begun to take effect, with same-sex marriage in Mexico finally legalized in 2022.

AÑO NUEVO

New Year's Eve *(Nochevieja)* is always a big deal in Mexico. While counting down to midnight might be the same here as it is around the world, there are a number of traditions and superstitions that make the celebration distinctly Mexican. Some of these can be traced back to Spain, including *"las doce uvas de la suerte"*, or the 12 lucky grapes. No one can say for certain when the tradition of eating 12 grapes on the stroke of midnight originated, but it's believed that the fruit brings good fortune for each month of the coming year. Lentils play a similarly symbolic role, with the coin-like shape of the legume thought to represent wealth and abundance. As with so many events in Mexico, food is central to the festivities, with vast portions of *pozole (p89)* and tamales *(p86)* served and dinner typically eaten late in the evening.

But, of course, New Year's Eve is predominately an excuse to gather together and have fun. The largest public celebration is in Mexico City, which sees a huge street festival centred around the main plaza, the Zócalo, as well as the monument known as the Ángel de la Independencia. Impromptu music fills the city, while queues form outside bars and nightclubs. As revellers gather for the final moments of the year, some might drop a gold ring into a glass of champagne before saying *"salud!"*, another symbol of good fortune.

Such celebrations demonstrate a firm commitment to the days ahead: the evening is a chance to remember past successes but, most importantly, to look forward to a brighter future. As the clock strikes midnight and fireworks illuminate the sky, a sense of optimism, faith and hope reigns. *¡Feliz Año Nuevo!*

INDEX

ACKNOWLEDGMENTS

DK Eyewitness would like to thank the following people for their contributions to this project: Nili Blanck, Rodrigo Rivero Borrell, Shakira Campion, Fabiola Mejia, Mariana Garcia, Sandra Irán Pradel Gutiérrez, Ramiro Maravilla, Pedro Velásquez Martínez, Amparo Rincón, Juan Diego Sandoval, Arturo Sosa, José Julio Villaseñor

Suzanne Barbezat fell in love with Oaxaca while travelling through Mexico in the late 1990s, and decided to make it her home. She shares her love of the country with others through her work as a writer and tour guide. Her book *Frida Kahlo at Home* (2016) explores the influences of the artist's surroundings on her life and work.

Lauren Cocking is a UK-born, Mexico-based writer, editor and translator who's called Mexico home for a decade. She's written about everything from the original Mexican energy drink to International Women's Day protests, but has a particular interest in Latin American literature by women authors. She's slowly inching her way to visiting all 32 of the country's states.

Luis F Domínguez is a freelance writer and independent journalist interested in travel, history and sport. He has written for *Sports Illustrated*, Fodor's, Yahoo! and Telemundo, among other brands of print and digital media in Europe and North America.

Mike Gerrard is a travel writer who also writes about his other love: spirits. He publishes the Travel Distilled website and is the author of *Cask Strength: The Story of the Barrel* (2023). He lives in southern Arizona, near the Mexico border, and has made many trips to the latter, in particular to explore the country's tequila distilleries.

Monica Galvan was born in Tijuana, Mexico and raised in San Diego, California. After majoring in Latin American Studies at the University of California, Los Angeles, she studied abroad in Mexico to hone her Spanish and to get to know her country of birth. Among other things, she's wandered through the colorful markets of Oaxaca and marveled at the ancient ruins of Chichen Itza.

Kana Kavon happily welcomed Mexico's strong imprint on her life at 16 years old when she volunteered in a Tzotzil village in Chiapas. She went on to teach the Spanish language for over a decade and has authored several publications, including a curriculum guide on Afro-Mexican history and culture.

Imogen Lepere is a travel and sustainability writer who specializes in stories about community tourism. She fell in love with Mexico while living in Nayarit and still visits regularly to top up her quota of cacao, creativity and artisan crafts. Her book *The Ethical Traveller* was published in 2022.

Oscar Lopez is a Mexican writer based in Mexico City, where he writes for outlets including *The Washington Post*, *The New York Times* and *The Guardian*. His work has received widespread recognition including a Livingston Award nomination, a Logan Nonfiction Fellowship and, most recently, a Radcliffe Fellowship from Harvard University.

Jennifer Fernández Solano is a writer and editor born and raised in Mexico City. She writes about travel, food and culture, mostly focusing on her native Mexico. Her writing has appeared in Lonely Planet, *Condé Nast Traveller*, *Forbes*, *The Independent* and *VinePair*, among other publications.

Carlos José Pérez Sámano is a socially committed writer that loves to share Mexican culture through his work. He is the Inaugural Artist in Residency at the University of Pennsylvania Museum of Archaeology and Anthropology. In addition, he is currently writing two opera librettos about decolonization with a Latin-American perspective.

Leigh Thelmadatter came to Mexico 20 years ago and was captivated. For most of that time, she's been involved in documenting Mexico's culture and life through student publications online, and later as a freelance writer. In 2019, her book *Mexican Cartonería: Paper, Paste and Fiesta* was published.

Ana Karina Zatarain is a Mexican writer and editor. She has written about Mexican culture for publications such as *The New Yorker*, *Vogue*, *GQ* and *PURPLE*. Having split her life between the US and Mexico, she is currently writing her debut book of essays on the cultural flux between both countries, to be published by Knopf in 2024.

Scarlett Lindeman is a chef, researcher and writer based in Mexico City. She was a doctoral candidate in sociology at CUNY's Graduate Center and has a masters degree in food studies. She is the chef and owner of Cicatriz and Ojo Rojo Diner.

Gerardo Mendiola Patiño is an editor of tourism and outreach books for children and young people. He studied economics at Universidad Nacional Autónoma de México (UNAM) and currently divides his activity between editing reports on climate change in Mexico and hiking.

About the illustrator:
Luis Pinto is an award-winning Mexican graphic designer and illustrator, who is influenced by everything from folk stories to graphic novels. He creates bright, colourful and expressive illustrations in a number of different mediums, and has worked with the likes of *EasyJet Traveller*, Google and *Little White Lies*, as well as Don Julio Tequila and Adobe.

PICTURE CREDITS

The publisher would like to thank the following for their kind permission to reproduce their photographs:

(Key: a-above; b-below/bottom; c-centre; f-far; l-left; r-right; t-top)

4Corners: Natalino Russo 158bl

AbeBooks: The Underdogs: A Novel Of The Mexican Revolution: Published By A Signet Classic / New American Library [1963], New York 177tr

Alamy Stock Photo: Album, David Alfaro Siqueiros, Echo of a Scream, Museum: © Museum of Modern Art, New York / © DACS 2024 165bl, Allstar Picture Library Ltd 149br, Archives du 7e Art collection, Photo 12 137tl, Jennika Argent 197tr, The Artchives, Frida Kahlo, Self-portrait with Thorn Necklace and Hummingbird © Banco de México Diego Rivera Frida Kahlo Museums Trust, Mexico, D.F./ © DACS 2024 165tr, Guy Bell, The Altar by Betsabeé Romero/ © DACS 2024 162-163tc, Judy Bellah 196bl, Marco Boldrin 20-21, Jennifer Booher 201t, Gregory Bull / Associated Press 139tr, Ruslan Bustamante 121br, Jair Cabrera / dpa / Alamy Live News 155tr, Cavan Images 60t, 215, Marcia Chambers 83tl, Diego Rivera's monumental stairway mural, National Palace, Palacio Nacional, Mexico City © Banco de México Diego Rivera Frida Kahlo Museums Trust, Mexico, D.F. / © DACS 2024 162tl, Cinematic, Anhelo Producciones 135t, Collection Christophel © Altavista Films / Zeta Film 137cl, Danita Delimont 85l, Mark Eden 170t, Richard Ellis 25t, 62-63, 98-99, 124t, 129tl, 203, Everett Collection Inc 132bl, Jon G. Fuller / VWPics 169tl, M. Garfat / MGP 112-113, Granger - Historical Picture Archive / Sor Juana Ines De La Cruz / N (1651-1695). Mexican Nun And Poet. Oil On Canvas By A Mexican Artist, C18th Century 177tl, Jeffrey Isaac Greenberg 173tr, Lindsay Lauckner Gundlock 85r, 88br, 90bl, 121tl, Christian Kober / Robert Harding 10tr, ML Harris 47, Hector Adolfo Quintanar Perez / ZUMA Press, Inc. 201b, Gardel Bertrand / Hemis.fr 129cr, Leroy Francis / Hemis.fr 128bl, Japhotos 69r, Robert Landau 94bl, Sébastien Lecocq 159t, Holger Leue / Image Professionals GmbH 72-73, Yueqi Li 183tr, Lifestyle pictures / Espectculos Flmicos El Coyl / Pimienta Films / Esperanto Filmoj 137br, Craig Lovell / Eagle Visions Photography 88bl, 202bl, Jon Lovette 87br, Jens Lucking / Cultura Creative Ltd 148t, Ludi 146br, Luis E Salgado / ZUMA Press, Inc. 204bl, Charles Mahaux / AGF Srl 116bl, Megapress Images 66br, Mier Y Brooks / Album 143t, Hugh Mitton 115t, Juan Carlos Muñoz 121bl, Luc Novovitch 204tr, Brian Overcast 54t, Panoramic Images 53tl, Ida Pap 174-175, Alejandro Paris / Majority World CIC 30, Lynnette Peizer / Stockimo 61, Karin Pezo 110bl, Slim Plantagenate 115br, Prisma Archivo 39t, Abraham Romero B. 56c, Adriana Rosas 71r, M. Sobreira 65, David South 23t, Dave Stamboulis 88tl, TCD / Prod.DB, © Avanti Pictures - Corpulenta Producciones 134br, TCD / Prod.DB, © Peliculas Rodriguez S.A. 133t, The History Emporium 42-43, Greg Vaughn 13, Eduardo Verdugo / Associated Press 205tr, 214bl, Jim West 154bl, 213, Adam Wiseman 91r, ZUMA Press, Inc. 71tl

Apple TV+: 140tr

AWL Images: Danita Delimont Stock 19tl, 19bl, Christian Heeb 12bl, Hemis 69bl, 87tr, 106t

Ballet Folklórico de México de Amalia Hernández: 10br, 153t

Bridgeman Images: © Christie's Images 50bl, Index Fototeca Diego Rivera, The Creation of Man, page from 'Popol Vuh' (w / c on paper): © Banco de México Diego Rivera Frida Kahlo Museums Trust, Mexico, D.F./ © DACS 2024 51t

© DACS 2024: Frida Kahlo, Self-portrait with Thorn Necklace and Hummingbird © Banco de México Diego Rivera Frida Kahlo Museums Trust, Mexico, D.F. 165tr, Diego Rivera, Man at the Crossroads, fresco, Rockefeller Center, New York. © Banco de México Diego Rivera Frida Kahlo Museums Trust, Mexico, D.F. 165tl, Diego Rivera, The Creation of Man, page from 'Popol Vuh' (w / c on paper): © Banco de México Diego Rivera Frida Kahlo Museums Trust, Mexico, D.F. 51t, Diego Rivera's monumental stairway mural, National Palace, Palacio Nacional, Mexico City © Banco de México Diego Rivera Frida Kahlo Museums Trust, Mexico, D.F. 162tl, The Altar by Betsabeé Romero 162-163tc, Rufino Tamayo, Three People, 1970. © D.R. Rufino Tamayo / Herederos / México / Fundación Olga y Rufino Tamayo, A.C./ ARS, NY and DACS, London 2024 165br, David Alfaro Siqueiros, Echo of a Scream, Museum: © Museum of Modern Art, New York 165bl

Diego & Kaito Cocina Tradicional Japonesa: 111tr

Dreamstime.com: Adalbertus 15, Belish 88cl, Costmo 87cl, Kobby Dagan 32cr, Jcfotografo 6t, 19cl, Sharon Jones 169tr, Madrugadaverde 67t, Kertu Saarits 48br, Dinorah Alejandra Arizpe Valds 16tr

Justin Foulkes: 14br

Getty Images: Gonzalo Azumendi 69br, Gale Beery 10bl, Bettmann 166-167, Cristopher Rogel Blanquet 206-207, Jose Castañares/ AFP / Stringer 70bl, Al Fenn 178bl, Marcos Ferro / Aurora Photos 19br, Fitopardo 16br, Cesar Gomez / Jam Media 155tl, Leonardo Alvarez Hernandez 179t, Sergio Mendoza Hochmann 11tl, Wolfgang Kaehler 59br, Wolfgang Kaehler / LightRocket 172bl, Keystone-France / Gamma-Keystone Diego Rivera, Man at the Crossroads, fresco, Rockefeller Center, New York. © Banco de México Diego Rivera Frida Kahlo Museums Trust, Mexico, D.F./ © DACS 2024 165tl, LMPC 137tr, Jon Lovette 26bl, Alfredo Martinez 119br, Mario Martinez 81t, Medios y Media 126tl, 126-127tc, 140tl, NurPhoto 52t, DEA / G. DAGLI ORTI 22t, Christopher Polk 130-131, Rawfile Redux 82t, Richard Ross 181t, Leopoldo Smith / Stringer 198-199, Jan Sochor 91tl, 104-105, Sexto Sol 185bl, Chip Somodevilla 75, Manuel Velasquez / Stringer 87tl, Jeremy Woodhouse 69cl

Getty Images / iStock: 185tr, Cinthia Aguilar 33tl, Alex Borderline 80t, Juan Carlos Castro 16bl, Drazen 210tr, Ferrantraite 7, 185cl, 186-187, FG Trade Latin 125tl, 191, Abel Gonzalez 49tl, Izanbar 16tl, Arturo Peña Romano Medina 69tl, Mgstudyo 16cl, MStudioImages 24bl, Chepe Nicoli 34-35, Jeremy Poland 100bl, Monica Rodriguez 109, Barna Tanko 173tl, THEPALMER 150-151

Netza Gramajo: Sak Tzevul 57r

IMCINE: Archive of the Mexican Film Institute 137bl

Mary Lagier: 31tr, 97l, 97r, 117t

Francesco Lastrucci: 11tr, 19tr, 59t, 95t, 192, 195, 211

Mathieu Richer Mamousse: 145

Johnny Miller / Unequal Scenes: 29t

Sandra Pereznieto: 183tl

RSM Design: Branding, Signage and Wayfinding: Miller Hull: Architect 77t

Shutterstock.com: Blackzheep 56bl, Luis A. Castillo 57tl, Marti Bug Catcher 216-217, Cinoq 106bl, Isabelle Clips 93, Ulises Ruiz Basurto / EPA-EFE 90tr, Natalia Esch 119bl, Gabonava 197tl, Sleepy Joe 40t, Raul Luna 209, Riiccardoperez 87bl, Arturo Verea 172cr

TelevisaUnivision: 140cl, 140bl, 140br

Unsplash: Carlos Aguilar 32bl, Alex Azabache 37, Juliana Barquero 185tl, Christian Coquet 102br, Priss Enri 110tr, Jorge Gardner 27, Zac Meadowcroft 101, Robert Penaloza 76b, Sean Quillen 103t, Jimmy Woo 33tr

Jerry Villagrana: 147t

wikiart.org: Rufino Tamayo, Tres Personajes, 1970 © D.R. Rufino Tamayo / Herederos / México / Fundación Olga y Rufino Tamayo, A.C./ ARS, NY and DACS, London 2024 / © DACS 2024 165br

Wikimedia Commons: Russ Bowling from Greenwood, SC, USA, CC BY 2.0 161tl, Gomnrz, CC BY 4.0 185br, Gzzz, CC BY-SA 4.0 121tr, Juan Carlos Fonseca Mata, CC BY-SA 4.0 160, Alejandro Linares Garcia, CC BY-SA 3.0 119tr, Miguel Angel Mandujano Contreras, CC BY-SA 4.0 196c, ProtoplasmaKid, CC BY-SA 4.0 88tr, Maritza Ros / Secretara de Cultura CDMX, CC BY 2.0 119tl

All other images © Dorling Kindersley

Project Editor Rachel Laidler
Editor Alex Pathe
Project Designer Claire Rochford
Senior Designer Laura O'Brien
Senior Editor Zoë Rutland
Proofreader Kathryn Glendenning
Indexer Helen Peters
Sensitivity Reader Jan de la Rosa
Senior Cartographic Editor James Macdonald
Picture Researcher Claire Guest
Illustrator Luis Pinto
Publishing Assistant Simona Velikova
Jacket Designer Sarah Snelling
Senior DTP Designer Tanveer Zaidi
Senior Production Editor Jason Little
Senior Production Controller Samantha Cross
Managing Editor Hollie Teague
Managing Art Editors Sarah Snelling, Gemma Doyle
Art Director Maxine Pedliham
Publishing Director Georgina Dee

First published in Great Britain in 2024
by Dorling Kindersley Limited
DK, One Embassy Gardens, 8 Viaduct Gardens,
London, SW11 7BW.

The authorised representative in the EEA is
Dorling Kindersley Verlag GmbH. Arnulfstr. 124,
80636 Munich, Germany.

Copyright © 2024 Dorling Kindersley Limited
A Penguin Random House Company
24 25 26 27 28 10 9 8 7 6 5 4 3 2 1
001-341531-Jun/2024

A CIP catalog record for this book is available from the British Library.
A catalog record for this book is available from the Library of Congress.

ISBN: 978 0 2416 7988 3

Printed and bound in China

www.dk.com

A note from the publisher
World events occur and policies and trends change or evolve at a rapid pace. Every effort has been made to ensure this book is accurate and up-to-date, so if you notice we've got something wrong or left something out, we want to hear about it. Please get in touch at travelguides@dk.com